Study Reading

A course in reading skills for academic purposes

Eric H. Glendinning
Beverly Holmström

LIVERPOOL
JOHN MOORES UNIVERSITY
AVRIL ROBARTS LRC
TEL. 0151 231 4022

PUBLISHED BY THE PRESS SYNDICATE OF THE UNIVERSITY OF CAMBRIDGE
The Pitt Building, Trumpington Street, Cambridge CB2 1RP, United Kingdom

CAMBRIDGE UNIVERSITY PRESS
The Edinburgh Building, Cambridge CB2 2RU, United Kingdom
40 West 20th Street, New York, NY 10011–4211, USA
10 Stamford Road, Oakleigh, Melbourne 3166, Australia

© Cambridge University Press 1992

This book is in copyright. Subject to statutory exception
and to the provisions of relevant collective licensing agreements,
no reproduction of any part may take place without
the written permission of Cambridge University Press.

First published 1992
Fifth printing 1997

Printed in the United Kingdom
by Scotprint Ltd, Musselburgh, Scotland

A catalogue record for this book is available from the British Library

ISBN 0 521 39974 2

LIVERPOOL
JOHN MOORES UNIVERSITY
AVRIL ROBARTS LRC
TITHEBARN STREET
LIVERPOOL L2 2ER
TEL. 0151 231 4022

Study Reading

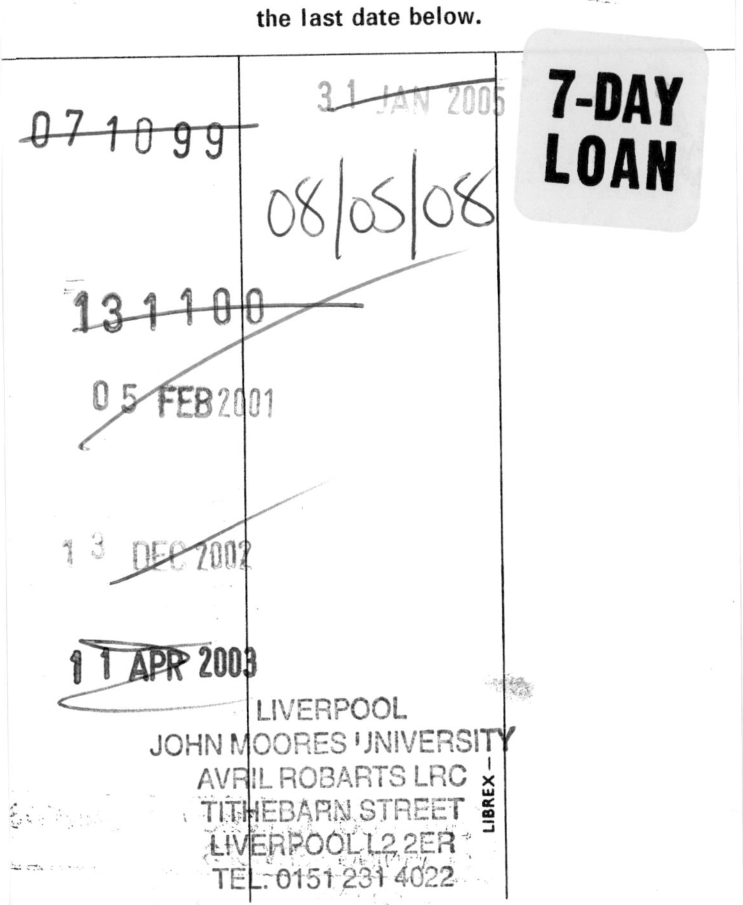

Books are to be returned on or before the last date below.

7-DAY LOAN

LIVERPOOL
JOHN MOORES UNIVERSITY
AVRIL ROBARTS LRC
TITHEBARN STREET
LIVERPOOL L2 2ER
TEL. 0151 231 4022

LIBREX

LIVERPOOL JMU LIBRARY
3 1111 00849 0227

ENGLISH FOR ACADEMIC PURPOSES titles from Cambridge

Study Skills in English *by Michael J. Wallace*

Study Listening – Understanding lectures and talks in English *by Tony Lynch*

Study Writing – A course in written English for academic and professional purposes *by Liz Hamp-Lyons and Ben Heasley*

Study Speaking – A course in spoken English for academic purposes *by Tony Lynch and Kenneth Anderson*

Study Reading – A course in reading skills for academic purposes *by Eric H. Glendinning and Beverly Holmström*

Contents

Thanks viii
To the student 1
To the teacher 3

PART 1 PREPARING TO STUDY

Unit 1 Getting to know your textbook 6
To make you think
Reading and interaction
Surveying a textbook
Scanning
Text exploration
Discourse study: Textbook structure
Word study: Words which substitute for other words
Grammar and meaning: Ellipsis
Application

Unit 2 Choosing what to read 16
To make you think
Reading and interaction
Reading with a purpose
Prediction
Text exploration
Discourse study: Chapter structure
Word study: Dealing with unfamiliar words
Application

PART 2 KNOWING WHAT'S IMPORTANT

Unit 3 The spirit of enquiry 30
To make you think
Reading and interaction
Surveying a text
Text exploration
Discourse study: Linking words
Word study: Using immediate context
Application

LIVERPOOL
JOHN MOORES UNIVERSITY
AVRIL ROBARTS LRC
TEL. 0151 231 4022

Unit 4 The developing world 41
To make you think
Reading and interaction
Reading for important points
Text exploration
Discourse study: Signpost expressions
Grammar and meaning: Focussing structures
Grammar and meaning: Cause and effect links
Word study: Word sets
Application

Unit 5 The natural world 54
To make you think
Reading and interaction
Making inferences
Note-taking: Linear notes
Text exploration
Discourse study: Identifying text structure
Word study: Word sets
Application

Unit 6 The physical world 66
To make you think
Reading and interaction
Reading graphics
Text exploration
Discourse study: Marking text structure
Discourse study: Note-taking – Spider notes
Word study: Using the wider context
Grammar and meaning: Hypothetical WOULD
Application

Unit 7 Into the future 84
To make you think
Reading and interaction
Comparing sources
Text exploration
Discourse study: Comparing text structures
Grammar and meaning: Degrees of certainty
Word study: Word structure
Application

Unit 8 The individual and society 94
To make you think
Reading and interaction
Critical reading
Text exploration
Discourse study: Forms of argument (1)
Grammar and meaning: Even if . . .
Word study: Maximisers and minimisers
Application

Unit 9 Work 104
To make you think
Reading and interaction
Critical reading: Comparing viewpoints
Text exploration
Discourse study: Forms of argument (2)
Word study: Emphasising and distancing
Application

PART 3 THE TOOLS OF RESEARCH

Unit 10 Using reference sources (1) 115
To make you think
Locating specific information
Choosing the best source
Comparing sources, comparing ideas

Unit 11 Using reference sources (2) 131
To make you think
Using a specialist index (1)
Using a specialist index (2)
Using abstracts

Key 146
Acknowledgements 165

Thanks

We are grateful to the following: Liz Hamp-Lyons for her advice in the initial stages of the project; past and present teachers of ELF, in particular Hazel O'Hara, Bryan Cruden and the 'Study Skills Faculty', namely Margie Ward, Diana Allan and Jim Littlejohn; colleagues at IALS for their helpful comments on early versions – Kenneth Anderson, David Hill, Tony Lynch, Jane Palfery and George Morrison.

We must thank too: centres in the UK and overseas who took part in the pilot study, in particular Barbara Duff and her colleagues in Oman; and our own students, who played such a large part in shaping this book.

For advice on sources, we would like to thank the staff of the Reference Section, Main Library, University of Edinburgh for help with Units 10 and 11; colleagues in many other departments for providing reading lists.

Well-deserved thanks to our editors, Elizabeth Serocold and Alison Silver, for encouragement, advice and fine judgement; Sheila and Mic for professional advice and for time to write.

Thanks to Stefania Guiducci for appearing on the cover.

To the student

Who is *Study Reading* for?

Study Reading is for students who have to use textbooks, reference materials and other sources written in English, for study purposes.

What does *Study Reading* cover?

Study Reading aims to develop the reading skills you need to find information quickly, to identify what is important in a text, and to compare different sources of information. To help you with these skills, we study how texts are structured, how grammar carries meaning, and how you can best deal with vocabulary problems.

Study Reading includes texts from the Humanities, Social Sciences and Science. Most of these texts are from sources used by college and university students in the English-speaking world. Some have been specially written to highlight particular reading problems. In *Part 1, Preparing to study*, we examine how textbooks are organised so that you can become familiar with the parts which will help you most. In *Part 2, Knowing what's important*, we study how to identify the important points in a text. Each unit provides a selection of texts on a theme important to the world of study. *Part 3, The tools of research*, provides help with the skills needed for research reading.

How does *Study Reading* work?

This book by itself cannot make you a better reader, but it can help you to think about how you read, compare ideas with your fellow students and experiment with different strategies. In this way, you can develop more efficient reading strategies for yourself.

Each unit has four sections. The first is to help you to think both about a reading skill and about the theme of the unit. The second provides reading practice and an opportunity to talk about your reading with your fellow students. The third explores some of the features of texts which can cause problems to the reader. Together, the first three sections should help you to develop and refine your reading skills. The fourth section allows you to apply your reading skills, old and new.

One piece of advice before you start this course – when you read, it is important that you have a clear purpose. Purposeful reading saves time for you to spend on other study activities. In this book, the instructions for each task indicate your reading purpose. When you study by yourself, you should set your own purpose. To develop faster reading, set yourself a time to achieve that purpose.

Good luck!

To the teacher

Who is *Study Reading* for?

Study Reading is aimed at two groups of readers: firstly, students preparing to enter or in the early stages of study at a college or university where English textbooks or reference materials are used but instruction is in the mother tongue; secondly, students at or preparing to enter English-medium colleges or universities. The book is intended for students whose English level is upper-intermediate.

What makes *Study Reading* different from other reading textbooks?

1. APPROACH *Study Reading* does not have a particular reading technique to sell. We recognise that students already have reading strategies in their own language and in English, however ineffectual these may be. The starting point is to give the reader insight into his or her existing strategies. The next step is to refine these strategies by exposure to the ideas of other students. Where students are working alone, this book encourages them to question their approach with the same aim of refining strategies. Only when the student has had time to think about reading in this way does the third stage follow, when we provide direct advice on improving reading efficiency.

2. METHODOLOGY *Study Reading* recognises that reading lessons can be dull if reading is seen as a passive activity. Consequently, a variety of problem-solving tasks are used to motivate students to think about reading. We have included a range of information and opinion-sharing activities in the belief that these will both motivate and help students to become better thinkers and readers by having to justify their answers to others.

3. TEXTS The texts are appropriate to the needs of students requiring reading skills for study purposes. *Study Reading* uses passages from textbooks, journals, reference works and study guides which have been drawn from current reading lists in a range of college and university disciplines and from a variety of higher education institutions. Care has been taken to select up-to-date sources or older sources which have become classic texts. US sources have been used as well as British to give students exposure to a wide variety of texts. Some texts have been constructed to highlight particular language points. Where possible, these

have been modelled, in terms of discourse structure, on authentic texts. Constructed texts have no source listed.

Theoretical influences

Study Reading has been shaped by classroom experience but has been influenced by theoretical debate. In the absence of any generally accepted theory of reading in a foreign language, we have selected such ideas from competing theories as have passed the classroom filter. The first two sections reflect Goodman's view of reading as a psycholinguistic guessing game (Goodman, 1967), whereas the third section includes bottom-up activities. Without subscribing to schemata theory, we accept the importance of knowledge of the world in reading and hence have attempted to activate the students' background knowledge using a variety of techniques. We accept too that knowledge of language is important and have therefore provided help with features of discourse and grammar. Our approach to vocabulary draws in part from the ideas of Nation and Coady on guessing from context (Nation and Coady, 1988).

How is *Study Reading* organised?

Study Reading is divided into three parts:

Part 1 Preparing to study
Part 2 Knowing what's important
Part 3 The tools of research

Part 1 (Units 1 and 2) This introduces basic reading skills which are returned to again and again throughout the book. The themes are 'Getting to know your textbook', and 'Choosing what to read'.

Part 2 (Units 3 to 9) This forms the main body of the book. Each unit is theme-based round a group of related subjects. For example, Unit 5, *The natural world*, draws texts from the life sciences. In this Part we study ways of identifying what is important in a text.

Part 3 (Units 10 and 11) This focusses on the reading skills required by students who have to prepare a project, dissertation or thesis. Unit 10 focusses on undergraduate reference sources, while Unit 11 is intended for postgraduate research students.

Each Part consists of a number of units. Each unit provides three to four hours of work and is divided into four sections:

Section 1 **To make you think** Tasks to develop insight into the reading process, engender discussion and provide a reason for reading on.

Section 2 **Reading and interaction** Information and opinion-sharing activities to encourage intensive reading and develop top-down reading skills.

Section 3 **Text exploration** Activities to develop bottom-up skills to make the reader aware of the common discourse features of academic texts, the role that grammar plays in conveying meaning, and strategies that can be used to tackle unfamiliar vocabulary.

Section 4 **Application** Tasks designed to encourage the reader to apply the strategies developed in the first three sections. These tasks are suitable for homework.

Study Reading ends with a *Key* to the tasks.

How can I use *Study Reading* with my class?

STUDY GROUP Each task is labelled 'Individual', 'Pairs' or 'Groups' and the instructions are clear. The most common work unit is the group. The size of the group will clearly depend on your teaching circumstances. About five or six per group would be ideal. If your students have adequate oral skills, encourage them to use English within their group. If their spoken English is poor and they have a mother tongue in common, allow discussion in the mother tongue. The important thing is to encourage the students to discuss and argue about their reading strategies. The *Key* should be used only when discussion has ended. It provides sample answers; other answers may also be acceptable. (This symbol 🗝 indicates that an answer is given in the *Key*.)

INFORMATION-GAP AND OPINION-GAP TASKS Throughout *Study Reading* there are tasks which ask students to read different sections of a long text or different texts on related themes. They then exchange information or opinions on the texts. Make sure the instructions are clearly understood. There is a natural tendency to read all of the texts. Encourage your students to do this *after* they have completed the activity.

PACING It is likely that students using this book will vary considerably in their reading proficiency. This means that some tasks may be missed out. There is no need to tackle every task in every unit. This is particularly the case with Units 1 and 2 where more proficient students may find some of the tasks quite simple. If so, move on quickly to more challenging material. You may also find that the discussion stage may make some of the later tasks redundant as students learn from each other. Given sufficient time, most students of the target level will be able to cope with all of the tasks. However, in real study situations time is at a premium. This is not a speed-reading course but it is important that students are encouraged to read quickly. Set a target by timing yourself and adding a proportion to match your students' abilities. Try reducing the proportion as you proceed through the book. The fourth section can be set for homework or self-study. Encourage your students to set themselves a target time for completing this work.

Goodman, K.S. (1967) Reading: a psycholinguistic guessing game, *Journal of the Reading Specialist*, 6, 4.

Nation, P. and Coady, J. (1988) Vocabulary and reading, in *Vocabulary and Language Teaching*, Carter, R. and McCarthy, M. (eds) (London: Longman).

LIVERPOOL
JOHN MOORES UNIVERSITY
AVRIL ROBARTS LRC
TEL. 0151 231 4022

PART 1 PREPARING TO STUDY

Unit 1 Getting to know your textbook

During your studies, you will learn from your lecturers, your fellow students and from books. Your textbook is one of your most valuable sources of information. It is important that you know how to use it effectively.

This unit aims to develop the reading skills required for:
1. surveying a textbook
2. using an index
3. dealing with word problems

TO MAKE YOU THINK

Task 1 (Individual, then pairs)

Knowing the parts of a textbook is the first step to using it properly. Study this list of some of the parts of a textbook. Try to match the parts with the correct descriptions.

Parts of a textbook	*Descriptions*
1. front cover	a) the units of the book
2. title page	b) sources used by the author
3. publishing details	c) a list of the main topics by chapter
4. preface/introduction	d) a page containing title and author's name
5. acknowledgements	e) an alphabetical list of topics in detail
6. contents	f) publisher, place and date of publication
7. chapters	g) selling points, author information, positive reviews
8. references	h) thanks to people who have helped with the book
9. glossary	i) the author's aims and the coverage of the book
10. index	j) a mini-dictionary of specialist terms used
11. back cover (or dust jacket blurb)	k) title, author and often an illustration in colour

When you have finished, compare your answers with your neighbour. Use your dictionary to find definitions for these parts:

appendix
bibliography
foreword

Task 2 (Individual, then pairs)

Identify these parts of a textbook (opposite). Then compare your answers with your neighbour.

A

plague, 84
planting dates, 31
poisonings, by insecticides, 51
poisons: contact, 17, 41–2, 43, 79;
tachnids, 62
tansy ragwort (*Senecio jacobea*), 80–1
taxonomy, necessity for, 7
temperature control, 37

B

1 Introduction 1
1.1 The origins of pests 1
1.2 Pest damage 2
1.3 The major types of pests 3

C

Tarsus (pl. tarsi) The jointed 'foot' that bears the claws of an insect.
Tergum (pl. terga) The dorsal body sclerite of an insect.
Thorax That portion of an insect's body which lies between the head and abdomen and bears the legs and wings.

D

Over the past 50 years a major portion of the world's population has been undernourished or starving. The World Bank has estimated that 65% of the people in developing countries receive at least 15% fewer calories than needed to function efficiently. This deficiency amounts

E

First published 1985

Published by *Macmillan Publishers Ltd*
London and Basingstoke
Associated companies and representatives in Accra, Auckland, Delhi, Dublin, Gaborone, Hamburg, Harare, Hong Kong, Kuala Lumpur, Lagos, Manzini, Melbourne, Mexico City, Nairobi, New York, Singapore, Tokyo

ISBN 0 - 333 - 39240 - X

F

An Introduction to Insect Pests and their Control

Peter D. Stiling

G

'I would certainly recommend the book for the courses for which it is written, as well as for higher courses as an introductory text.'
Dr. T.H. Coaker, Department of Applied Biology, University of Cambridge.

Introduction to Insect Pests and their Control is written for certificate, diploma and degree courses in agriculture, applied biology and zoology. It will also find a place in 'A' level biology and agriculture courses, and as a supplement to medical entomology courses.

Stiling, P.D. (1985) *An Introduction to Insect Pests and their Control* (London: Macmillan).

Task 3 (Individual)

Why do you think you should read these parts of a textbook? Note your reasons for reading each part.

1. cover or dust jacket
2. title page
3. publishing details
4. foreword, preface or introduction
5. table of contents
6. index
7. bibliography

Task 4 (Individual, then groups)

Study this passage to find the reasons given for reading each of the textbook parts listed in Task 3.

Discuss with the others in your group any differences between your answers to Task 3 and the reasons given in the passage.

> Before accepting information published in a book, you should spend a few minutes examining its structure, for this will assist you in evaluating the book. The dust-jacket often contains information on the qualifications of the author and his point-of-view. Allowance must, of course, be made for the natural desire of the publisher and author to present the book in its best light. The title page should always be read carefully. It may contain a sub-title explaining the intention or scope of the work, or the qualifications of the author. The imprint (place of publication, publisher and date) is of value. The work is likely to be authoritative if published by a publisher who specializes in the subject of the book. The date will indicate how up-to-date the book is and the reverse of the title page should also be examined, in case this reveals whether the edition is substantially a reprint of an older work. The foreword, preface or introduction will often summarize the purpose of the volume (see Fig. 53). The table of contents will not only outline the way the work is arranged and help you to trace a particular piece of information (see Fig. 28) if the index is defective, but will also suggest the point-of-view. Every book is based on a combination of objective facts and subjective interpretation of them. The contents will suggest whether the author has set out to prove a theory or to spread a particular belief. The book may be of great value even if it contains propaganda, but greater care must be taken in evaluating the information. The running headlines on the top of the pages may contain useful information on the text. The index can reveal the scope of the book by listing the topics discussed (see Fig. 54) and the number of pages devoted to them. It can also reveal bias by the number of references under particular topics. The bibliography will reveal the author's sources and will indicate whether he is up-to-date and thorough in his approach.

Chandler, G. (1982) *How to Find Out, Printed and On-Line Sources*, 5th edition, pp. 1–2 (Oxford: Pergamon Press).

READING AND INTERACTION

Surveying a textbook

'Surveying' means reading for the general idea. When you buy or borrow a textbook required for your course, it is useful to survey it to find out as quickly as you can how it is organised, the topics it covers, its level and any special features it has. It is also worth checking that the book is up-to-date by noting the date of publication and the edition. Check if there is a more up-to-date edition available before you borrow it. Noting the title, author and publication details is also worth doing, so that you can refer to the book in your written work and locate it easily in the library if you wish to borrow it again.

Task 5 (Individual, then groups)

This form can be used to make a quick survey of a textbook. Which of the parts you looked at in Task 1 would help you most to complete each section?

Discuss your ideas in your group.

1. Title ....
2. Author(s) or editor(s) ....
3. Publisher, date and place of publication ....
4. Edition ....
5. Level ....
6. Aims ....
7. Main topics covered ....
8. Special features ....

Task 6 (Individual)

Look through a textbook, preferably in your own subject, but which is unfamiliar to you. Try to survey the book in about 15 minutes. Use this book if you cannot get a textbook in your own subject.

Scanning

The index of your textbook is a useful key to information. 'Scanning' is one of the reading skills you require to locate information quickly in the index. 'Scanning' means reading to find specific information. You have a specific target and you search the text for the words which match the information you need.

Given enough time, anyone can find information in an index. The important thing is to find the information you want as quickly as possible. To do this, you should let your eye go up and down the index columns until you find the references beginning with the correct letters. Then focus more finely to search for the specific references you want. With practice, you can become faster at scanning by narrowing the area you scan – moving from coarse to fine focus – as quickly as possible.

Task 7 (Individual, then pairs)

Scan the index on page 11 to find information on the following. Write only the page number. Where more than one page number is given in the index, indicate the page or pages you would refer to first. **Bold** type in this index indicates an illustration. Work as quickly as you can.

Warning! You will not be able to find a reference to one of these topics.

1. Sir Isaac Newton's *Principia*
2. John von Neumann's book on computers
3. Sir Charles Lyell's *The Principles of Geology*
4. The French Revolution (1789)
5. Ernest Rutherford's appearance
6. The life of Paracelsus
7. The oxygenation of blood
8. The theorem of Pythagoras
9. The Natural History Society, Brno
10. The architecture of Ancient Rome

When you have found your answers, compare with another student.

Sometimes we cannot find the information we want in an index, although the book may contain all the information we need. If you cannot find your topic, make sure first that you are using the correct key word. The most likely key words in these examples are in **bold** type:

The discovery of **oxygen**
Sir Isaac **Newton**'s interest in the occult

Often more than one key word is possible. For example, 'The architecture of Ancient Rome' may be listed in an index as:

Rome, Ancient, architecture of

or

Architecture, of Ancient Rome

If you cannot find a very specific reference, try a more general key word. For example, to find The French Revolution of 1789 you may have to try any of the terms in **bold** type:

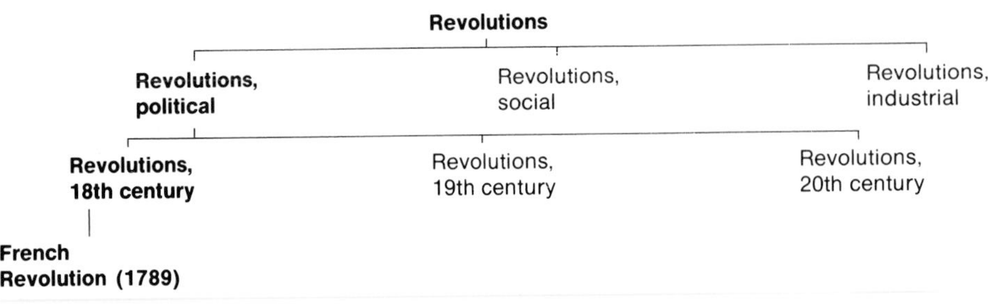

Index

1821), 268
Napoleon III, emperor of France (1808–73), 311
Navigation, **115**, 192, 194, 224, 239, 241, 243, 262
Neanderthal Man, 41, 46
Nervi, Pier Luigi, (1891), *Palazetto dello Sport, Rome*, **46**
Neumann, John von (1903–57), **204**, **217**, 432–6; *Theory of Games and Economic Behaviour*, 432–3; *The Computer and the Brain*, 433
Neutron, 341, 351, 369
Newton, Sir Isaac (1642–1727), **109**, 184, 218, 221–43, 254, 259, 332, 334, 336, 337, 412, 437; and Calculus, 184, 222, 223, 233; at Cambridge, **104**, 223, 224, 233; at the Mint, **107**, **111**, 234, 236; at Woolsthorpe, 218, 221–3, 233; occult, interest in, 234; work on *Opticks*, **106**, **111**, 223–8, 332; work on the *Principia*, **108**, 233
Nicholas II, tsar of Russia (1868–1918), 326
Nomadic way of life, **21**, 60, 61, 62, 69, 86, 162, 165
Numerals, evolution of modern system, 168, 177

Oak Ridge National Laboratory, Tennessee, **169**, 341–43, 349
Olduvai Gorge, Tanzania, 28–9
Oljeitu Khan (ruled 1304–16), **33**, 80, 86, 89
Omo Valley, Ethiopia, **4**, 24–9, 438
Orgel, Leslie Eleazer (1927), **155**, 314, 316
Ostwald, Wilhelm (1853–1932), 351
O'Sullivan, T. H. (1840–82), *Photographs of Landscape*, **35**
Oxygen, discovery of, 148, 150; in air, 148; in blood, 32; in DNA, 390; in primitive atmosphere, 314; in universe, 344; oxides of mercury, 123; phlogiston theory, 142, 150

Paestum, Southern Italy, **39**, 104–106
Paine, Thomas (1737–1809), **130**, 272; *The Rights of Man*, 272–3
Paracelsus, Aureolus Philippus Theophrastus Bombastus von Hohenheim (1493–1541), **58**, **59**, **60**, 123, 139–44, 321
Pascal, Blaise (1623–62), 424
Pasteur, Louis (1822–95), **152**, **154**, **204**, 311–13
Paul III, Pope (1468–1549), 209
Pauling, Linus (1901), 392
Peking man, *see Homo erectus*
Pepys, Samuel (1633–1703), 233
Perspective studies, **76**, **77**, **78**, **79**, **80**, 179–84, 196
Physics, history of, 110, 125, 165, 221–56, 321–74, 411, 436
Picasso, Pablo (1881–1973), *Les Demoiselles d'Avignon*, *Portrait of Daniel-Henry Kahnweiler*, 332
Pisano, Andrea (c.1290–1348), *The Creation of Woman*, **199**
Pizarro, Francisco (c. 1470–1541), 101
Plague, The, 222, 223, 229, 280
Planck, Max Karl Ernst Ludwig (1858–1947), 336, 351, 365
Planets, paths of, **85**, **102**, **165**, 156, 157, 164, 165, 194, 196, 197, 204, 211, 221, 244, 318, 334, 351, 358, 360
Plasma Physics, 349
Plato (428–348 BC), 425
Plough, invention of, **27**, 74, 79
Polycrates (d.c. 522 BC), 155
Pope, Alexander (1688–1744), *Lines written in Windsor-Forest*, 228
Priestley, Joseph (1733–1804), **61**, 144–8, 274, 277
Proconsul africanus, also known as *Dryopithecus africanus*, **10**; 36, 38, 42
Protein structure, 76, 348; adenine in, **157**, 316, 318; evolution of, 316; in haemoglobin, 309; in myoglobin, 314; *see also* Deoxyribonucleic acid (DNA)
Ptolemy, Claudius (2nd century AD), **70**, 164, 184, 194, 196–8, 204, 208–9; *Almagest*, 177
Pueblo Tribes, Arizona, **36**, 92–6
Pyramids, 112, 131, 158, 349
Pythagoras (c. 570–500 BC), **66**, **67**, **68**, 104, 155–62, 172–3, 187, 223, 234; Theorem, 156–62, 173, 339

Qanats, Khuzistan, 77
Quipu, **38**, 100, 101

Ramapithecus punjabicus, **10**, 38
Raphael, Santi (1483–1520), 424
Rashid al-Din, *Jami' al-Tawarikh*, **30**, 80
Reformation, the, and Counter-Reformation, 141, 142, 205, 206, 207, 221, 222
Renaissance, 177–184, 197, 208, 286; moves to Northern Europe, 221, 424, 425, 426
Revolutions, Industrial, **124**, **137**, 259–88; scientific, 218, 221; 17th-century, 221–2; 18th-century, 144, 148, 259–72; 19th-century, 379
Rheims Cathedral, France, **43**; **45**, 109–12
Rift Valley, East Africa, 25, 72
Rodia, Simon (1879–1965), 118–21; *The Watts Towers*, **49**, 121
Röntgen, Wilhelm Konrad (1843–1923), **177**, 332, 356
Rome, Ancient, culture and architecture of, 109, 110, 160, 274, 435, 437
Roosevelt, Franklin Delano (1882–1945), **184**, 370
Rousseau, Jean-Jacques (1712–78), 424
Rudolf, Lake, Kenya, Ethiopia, 25, 29
Ruskin, John (1819–1900), *The Stones of Venice*, 109
Russell, Bertrand (1872–1970), 254
Rutherford, Ernest, First Baron (1871–1937), **163**, **166**, 328, 334–7, 351, 368
Rysbrack, John Michael (1693?–1770), *Isaac Newton Monument, Westminster Abbey*, **109**, **111**

Sacchi, Andrea (1599–1661) **97**, 211
Salk Institute for Biological Studies, San Diego, California, **210**, 367, 370, 393, 419
Sanchez, Robert (1938), **155**, 314
Schelling, Friederich Wilhelm Joseph von (1775–1854), *Naturphilosophie*, 282, 285
Schrödinger, Erwin (1887–1961), 329, 362, 367
Scientific societies: Academy of Sciences, St Petersburg, 330; Accademia Cimento, Rome, 198; British Association for the Advancement of Science, 368; Lincean Society, Rome, **92**; Linnean Society, London, 308; Lunar Society of Birmingham, 277–80; Manchester Literary and Philosophical Society, 150–3; Natural History Society, Brno, 385; Royal Society of London, 226, 227, 233, 254, 412, 259, 271, 277
Selkirk, Alexander (1676–1721), 192
Seurat, Georges (1859–91), *Young Woman with a Powder Puff, Le Bec*, **164**, 332
Shakespeare, William (1564–1616), 228, 437; *Hamlet*, 424; *King Lear*, 360; *Othello*, 198; *The Merchant of Venice*, 198; *The Tempest*, 156
Sharples, Ellen (c.1790), *Pastel portrait of Joseph Priestley*, **61**
Skinner, Burrhus Frederic (1904), 412
Socrates (470–399 BC), 362, 427, 429
Sophocles (c. 496–406 BC), *Electra*, 197

447

Bronowski, J. (1973) *Ascent of Man*, p. 447 (London: British Broadcasting Corporation).

Task 8 (Individual)

Match each of the topics (1–10) from a geography textbook with a more general key word (a–j) from the index.

Topic	*Index key word*
1. air routes	a) ores
2. cultivation of oranges	b) urbanisation
3. troposphere	c) sea routes
4. cotton growing	d) mining
5. underpopulation	e) transportation
6. Panama Canal	f) climate
7. growth of New York	g) atmosphere
8. uranium	h) population
9. coal production	i) industrial crops
10. rainfall	j) citrus farming

TEXT EXPLORATION

Discourse study: Textbook structure

A typical textbook has this structure:

Introduction

Contents

Chapters
1.
2.
3.
etc.

Further reading

Appendices

Index

The best guide to the organisation of the textbook and the topics it covers is provided by the introduction and the contents. Pay particular attention to any section of the introduction labelled 'Advice to the reader', 'To the student', 'How to use this book', etc. You can safely ignore the acknowledgements.

Word study: Words which substitute for other words

In this section we will explore some of the features of written English which can cause problems for readers. Words are one of the first problems that readers face – words which are unfamiliar, words which substitute for other words, and words which appear to be missing. Here we will study ways of dealing with words which substitute for other words.

Writers often use different words in a text to refer to the same thing – the meaning remains the same but the words change. Study these examples:

1. Before accepting information published in *a book*, you should spend a few minutes examining its structure. *The work* is likely to be authoritative if published by a publisher who specializes in the subject of the book. The foreword, preface or introduction will often summarize the purpose of *the volume*.

Work and *volume* do not signal new topics. They are simply different words for *book* in this text. If you meet an unexpected change of topic in your reading, look back in the text. The writer may be using a new word for an old topic.

2. *The index* can reveal the scope of the book by listing *the topics* discussed and the number of pages devoted to *them*. *It* can also reveal bias by the number of references under particular topics.

Nouns change to pronouns, as in this example. If you have difficulty with a pronoun, look back in the text to find the noun referred to.

Grammar and meaning: Ellipsis

Words which appear to be missing may also cause problems. Some structures allow writers to omit words to avoid unnecessary repetition. Study these examples:

1. It is important that you have a clear purpose when you read. If not, you may waste valuable study time.
2. It is important that you have a clear purpose when you read. If *you do* not *have a clear purpose*, you may waste valuable study time.

Compare:

3. Dictionaries and encyclopaedias are important information sources. Both can be found in the reference section of your library.
4. Dictionaries and encyclopaedias are important information sources. Both *dictionaries and encyclopaedias* can be found in the reference section of your library.

Compare:

5. In addition to card catalogues, most libraries have on-line catalogues. On-line are more flexible than printed.
6. In addition to card catalogues, most libraries have on-line catalogues. On-line *catalogues* are more flexible than printed *catalogues*.

Task 9 (Individual)

Study this preface from a reference book. Answer the questions in italics about words which substitute for other words or appear to be missing.

> This book has been prepared to provide a guide to sources of information on engineering and its various branches. It *What does It refer to?* should prove of interest to all persons engaged in the engineering profession and those *Add the missing word* contemplating entering the *Add the missing word* profession. It is hoped that Chapters 1 and 8, on careers, and education and training, will assist both advisers and potential students seeking information about these important matters. *Which important matters?* This book has been arranged according to the Dewey Decimal Classification that is commonly employed in public libraries. Although the work *Which work?* is reasonably comprehensive, there are so many textbooks available that it has not been possible to make specific recommendations. *Of what? Add the missing words.* This matter *Which matter?* is better dealt with by tutors and others concerned with teaching. However, in certain chapters, selected books have been mentioned in addition to reference books and the like *The like of what?* when it has been felt that the details *Details of what?* would augment the general information provided. *Information provided where?* A number of the books referred to contain neither bibliographies nor guides to further reading.
>
> Parsons, S.A.J. (1972) *How to find out about engineering*, p. xiii (Oxford: Pergamon Press).

APPLICATION

Task 10 (Individual)

Study this extract from a study skills guide. Which chapters in the guide will provide help with these problems?

1. planning essays
2. acquiring basic study skills
3. setting out references
4. finding suitable books
5. preparing for examinations
6. looking for a job

> **How to Read this Book**
>
> There are seven chapters in the book, arranged in a sequence which roughly mirrors a student's progress through college. The first chapter deals with 'Starting off in higher education' and is intended mainly for people who are just about to go to university/college or who are in their first year there. If you are an experienced student, you may still find it useful to read this chapter fairly quickly.

The next three chapters tackle different aspects of normal coursework. Chapter 2 deals with 'Generating information', finding literature, using it effectively, and making notes. Chapter 3 describes 'Analysing concepts and theories', particularly explaining how to place problem concepts within a whole field of ideas. Once you have gathered enough information and you understand the major concepts involved in an area, Chapter 4 moves on to 'Writing essays'. It describes how to de-bug essay topics, plan your response, and write up finished text.

The next two chapters relate to course assessment. You may move on in your final year to 'Writing dissertations', the subject of Chapter 5. Dissertations pose some problems over and above ordinary essay writing, especially in organizing research, writing up a longer piece of text and referencing sources. Chapter 6 deals with the final and most critical stage in most courses, 'Revising for exams' and answering exam questions.

Chapter 7 on 'Turning study skills into life skills' is likely to be of immediate relevance if you are beginning the 'milk round' of career interviews and job applications. However, it is worth reading well in advance of this stage, since by then it is generally rather late to do anything about acquiring career-relevant skills. The earlier you think through some ideas about possible career lines, the greater the opportunity you have to undertake relevant activities and develop key personal qualities.

Dunleavy, P. (1986) *Studying for a Degree in the Humanities and Social Sciences*, pp. 1, 2 (London: Macmillan Education Ltd).

Unit 2 Choosing what to read

As a student you will find that there is always too much to read. It is important therefore that you can quickly select the most appropriate source for your needs. To do this, you must have a clear purpose for your reading and you must be able to predict which source will help you most.

This unit aims to develop the reading skills required for:

1. making predictions about your reading
2. surveying a chapter
3. dealing with unfamiliar words

TO MAKE YOU THINK

Task 1 (Individual, then groups)

Study this list of books on study skills. Which book would you refer to if you were:

1. A student worried about a forthcoming examination
2. A postgraduate wanting advice on how to prepare a thesis
3. A student who wanted advice on all aspects of study
4. A student preparing for a BA in sociology
5. A postgraduate about to do a classroom based project on learning techniques
6. A student who has problems remembering what she reads
7. A mature student going to college for the first time

Discuss your ideas in your group.

Borg, W.R. & Gall, M.D.	*Educational Research*, 5th ed., Longman, New York, 1989
Brown, M.	*How to Study Successfully for Better Exam Results*, Sheldon Press, London, 1990
Dunleavy, P.	*Studying for a Degree in the Humanities and Social Sciences*, Macmillan Education Ltd, London, 1986
Higbee, K.L.	*Your Memory, How it Works and How to Improve it*, Prentice-Hall, Englewood Cliffs, New Jersey, 1977
Maddox, H.	*How to Study*, Pan Books, London, 1988
Phillips, E.M. & Pugh, D.S.	*How to get a Ph.D.*, Open University Press, Milton Keynes, 1987
Rowntree, D.	*Learn How to Study, a guide for students of all ages*, 3rd ed., Macdonald Illustrated, London, 1988

Task 2 (Individual, then groups)

Study these contents pages from *Learn How to Study*. Which chapter and which section would you consult if you wanted help with these questions?

1. How do I learn to read faster?
2. How do I find out about assessment in my course?
3. How do I overcome anxiety about examinations?
4. What is the best way to take notes from a lecture?
5. How can I best timetable my studies?
6. What is the best way to revise for examinations?
7. What does my tutor expect when he or she sets an essay with the title, 'Account for . . .'?
8. How do I become a successful student?

Discuss your ideas in your group.

Contents

Preface
Please read this FIRST vii

1 *The myths and realities of being a student*
Doubts and uncertainties 1
The myth of the super-student 2
The secrets of success? 5

2 *Studying and learning*
Why are you studying? 8
What do you mean by learning? 14
What do you do when you're learning? 19
Making your own knowledge 28

3 *Understanding your situation*
The social climate 31
The learning climate 34
The assessment system 39

4 *Getting organized for learning*
What needs organizing? 49
Lifestyle 51
Learning resources 56
Organizing your time 62
Organizing your study sessions 67

5 *Developing a strategy for reading*
Managing your reading 72
SQ3R — a flexible strategy 76
SQ3R in lectures, etc.? 93

6 *The art of reading actively*
Looking for the main ideas 97
Picking out the details 100
Evaluating the text 107
Concentration and speed 109

7 *Learning from lectures and other listening*
Are you listening? 111
Learning in lectures 112
Learning in small groups 119
Tutorless groups 126

8 *Making and using notes*
Why make notes? 128
When do you make notes? 131
Three ways of writing notes 132
Notes in different circumstances 137
The physical appearance of your notes 143
Storing and using notes 145

9 *Writing essays and assignments*
The value of writing essays 148
Understanding the context 151
Analysing your task 153
Researching your raw material 156
Planning your essay 160
Writing your essay 165
Critiquing your essay 168
Learning from tutor feedback 171
Glossary of essay terms 175

10 *Dealing with examinations*
How do you feel about exams? 179
Putting anxiety in its place 182
Preparing for examinations 184
In the examination room 197
After the examination 203

Bibliography 207

Index 210

Rowntree, D. (1988) *Learn How to Study, a guide for students of all ages*, 3rd edition, pp. v–vi (London: Macdonald Illustrated).

Task 3 (Individual, then groups)

Study this text. Which lines would you refer to for help with each of these problems? Note the line numbers for each problem.

1. What source will provide me with explanations of the important ideas in my subject?
2. What source will provide help with all the social sciences?

Discuss your ideas in your group.

Acquiring some General Study Resources

Your first few months in higher education normally produce a dramatic broadening of your academic horizons. Unfamiliar concepts and arguments can easily go over your head, especially if you do not know where to follow them up. Even if you conscientiously make a note of ideas or labels you do not understand, many of your normal sources, even major textbooks, will either use concepts without defining them explicitly, or refer cryptically to patterns of argument or '-isms'. To cope with these problems, some general study resources are worth acquiring, while others can be followed up in libraries. Particularly useful are the following.

(a) **A specialist 'dictionary'** for your subject. These are available cheaply in paperback in all the humanities and social science disciplines and it is a good idea to make sure you have a personal copy. Recent second-hand copies are usually quite acceptable. Appendix 1 lists the good dictionaries currently in print in each of the humanities and social science subjects. Specialist subject dictionaries generally explain not only theoretical approaches but also key concepts, the contribution of major authors and central empirical controversies.

(b) **A more general reference book to academic disciplines** such as *The Fontana Dictionary of Modern Thought* (1983) – which provides very short explanations of twentieth-century schools of thought in many different subjects – or its sister volume the *Biographical Companion* (1983). Sources such as these can be quite affordable and are particularly useful in trying to understand trans-disciplinary perspectives.

(c) **Reference works covering a number of related academic disciplines** are worth consulting in libraries. Across all the social sciences the multi-volume *International Encyclopaedia of the Social Sciences* (1968) provides authoritative essays on theories, concepts and problems in the major disciplines. All college libraries and the biggest public libraries should have a copy in their reference sections. There is no comparable source for the humanities as a group, but Appendix 1 indicates some useful comprehensive sources available in the different humanities disciplines.

Dunleavy, P. (1986) *Studying for a Degree in the Humanities and Social Sciences*, pp. 13–14 (London: Macmillan Education Ltd).

The text above contains 37 lines. How many of them provided help with the first problem? How many of these lines were not relevant to either of your problems? What proportion of the text could you ignore?

READING AND INTERACTION

Reading with a purpose

When you read, it is important that you have a clear purpose. Having a clear purpose helps you to narrow the choice of book from a reading list and the best chapter and section to choose once you have selected the most appropriate textbook. Having a clear purpose also helps you to locate the most useful part of a text for your needs and to ignore those parts which will not help you.

Prediction

'Prediction' means making intelligent guesses about what a textbook, chapter or section contains using only a small sample of the text. It is an important skill when choosing what to read. The more we know about our subject, the easier it is for us to make predictions because we can relate the samples of new text to our existing knowledge. When our knowledge of the subject is limited, we have to make maximum use of all available clues to predict well. Study this example:

Which of these three chapters from a geography textbook will provide information on how the landscape of coastal regions is formed?

5. The Structure of the Continents
6. The Landscape and the River
7. Wave, Wind, and Ice

Chapter 5 is unlikely. It seems to be about the formation of continents. Chapter 6 contains the word *landscape*, but also *river*. Its topic is the way rivers shape the land, whereas our need is for information on how the coast is shaped. In other words, how the sea shapes the land. Chapter 7 contains the word *wave* – that suggests the sea. It follows a chapter about the formation of landscape by rivers and may therefore continue with other aspects of landscape formation. For these reasons, we can predict that Chapter 7 will include information on how the sea shapes the land and hence how the landscape of coastal regions is formed.

Task 4 (Individual, then pairs)

Look at the table of contents on page 21. In which chapter would you expect to find information on the following? Write only the number of the chapter.

1. The location of the world's major steel industries
2. The density of population in China
3. Rice production
4. Shipping routes
5. The influence of geology on city sites
6. Fertility of boulder clay
7. Japanese manufacturing belt
8. Eskimo hunting habits
9. Temperate humid climates

Compare your ideas with your neighbour.

Contents

PREFACE

INTRODUCTION: The Field of Geography - - - 1

I The Position of a Place - - - 8
II Shape and Size: Projections and Scales - 19
III Bedrock and Build - - - - 35
IV The Structure of the Continents (I) - - 54
V The Structure of the Continents (II) - 73
VI The Landscape and the River - - 84
VII Wave, Wind, and Ice - - - - 103
VIII Climate as a Geographic Factor - - 127
IX The Elements of Climate - - - 142
X Chief Climatic Regions of the World - - 165
XI Life Zones - - - - - 198
XII The Principal Life Zones - - - 214
XIII The Geography of Soils - - - 240
XIV Natural, Human, and Geographic Regions - 261
XV World Population - - - - 277
XVI Man in Humid Tropical Lands - - 294
XVII Man in Temperate Humid Lands - - 311
XVIII Man in Dry and Cold Lands - - - 328
XIX World Agriculture - - - - 347
XX Primary Production Other than Agriculture - 364
XXI The Geography of Manufacturing - - 384
XXII The Geography of Manufacturing: Heavy and Light Industries - - - - 406
XXIII Leading Industrial Regions of the World - 422
XXIV Geography and Transportation - - 436
XXV Geography and Rural Settlement - - 461
XXVI Urban Geography: the Urban World - - 478
XXVII Urban Geography: Factor of Local Site - 492
XXVIII Urban Geography: Purpose and Place - 508
XXIX Urban Geography: Function and Form - 525

INDEX

Wreford Watson, J. (1957) *General Geography*, Contents page (Mississauga: Copp Clark Publishing Company Ltd).

When you have selected a suitable textbook and identified the chapters most appropriate to your needs, it is useful to see what help is given in each chapter to enable you to read it effectively.

Task 5 (Individual, then groups)

This list shows some common chapter features. How can these features help you when you are reading a chapter?

1. Title
2. Introduction
3. Section headings
4. Subsection headings
5. Highlighted words
6. Diagrams and illustrations (graphics)
7. Summary
8. Suggestions for further reading
9. Problems
10. Notes/References

Discuss your selection in your group.

Task 6 (Groups)

Work in groups, A and B.

Group A
Study this chapter introduction from a study guide. The chapter is called 'Examinations'. What questions do you think this chapter will answer? Make a list of at least four questions. Compare your list with others in your group.

> All tests and examinations are intended to measure how effectively you have studied a subject, so the best way of preparing for examinations is to develop systematic habits of study. If you follow the advice which has already been given about methods of planning, note-taking, and learning effectively, you should have no difficulty with examinations.
>
> There is no way of passing an examination without doing the requisite work for it. But you can ensure that you are at peak efficiency for an important examination. This means having a thorough knowledge of your subject and having it so well organized and understood that you can write about it from many points of view. It also means being reasonably calm and confident, and not fatigued or over-anxious.
>
> Taking these things for granted, you can improve your performance still more by (1) careful preparation and (2) skill in examination techniques.
>
> Maddox, H. (1988) *How to Study*, p. 137 (London: Pan Books).

Group B
Study this chapter summary (opposite) from a study guide. The chapter is called 'Examinations'. What questions were answered in the chapter? Make a list of at least four questions. Compare your list with others in your group.

Summary

Preparations for examinations should begin at the outset of a course of study, in the sense that you should study the syllabus you are required to cover and the kinds of examinations which you will have to take.

Progressive assessment is now widely used to monitor course performance. Hence final examinations are less of an ordeal. Nevertheless fairly frequent tests and reviews are desirable. Little effort is required to relearn for an important examination what has already been gone over a number of times. To be most effective, review should follow closely on the original learning. For long-term retention intermediate periods of review are also desirable.

The final review preceding important examinations should be carefully planned to a schedule, to avoid any last-minute rush. Examination anxiety can be avoided by regular work, careful planning, and a normal routine which allows for exercise and recreation.

Different kinds of examinations require different kinds of preparation. Suggestions are offered for taking objective tests and for taking essay-type examinations.

Maddox, H. *op. cit.*, p. 155.

Task 7 (Groups)

Groups A and B

Now study this list of section headings from the same chapter. Think again about your list of questions. Do you want to change any of them? Agree on a common list with your group.

Preparing for examinations
Revision
Methods of revision
Avoiding anxiety
Form of examinations
Objective tests
Intelligence quotients
Techniques for essay-type examinations
Making use of returned papers
Summary

Maddox, H. *op. cit.*, pp. 136–56.

Task 8 (Pairs)

Work in pairs, one from Group A and one from Group B.

Compare your questions. How similar are they? Read each other's texts. Which parts provided the most help in making accurate questions?

TEXT EXPLORATION

Discourse study: Chapter structure

A typical textbook chapter has this structure:

Title
Introduction
Sections
1.
2.
3.
etc.
Summary
Further reading

Graphics

The best guide to the organisation of the chapter and the topics it covers is provided by the introduction and the section headings. Using these, you can predict the topics covered. You can check your predictions using the summary. Summaries can help you in two other ways. They can provide a quick overview of the whole chapter before you read it. They can also provide a useful comprehension check after you've read the chapter. If time is short, read the summary instead of the whole chapter. Refer back to the chapter for help with any points you cannot understand. Graphics sometimes provide easy-to-read summaries of sections. See Task 15.

Word study: Dealing with unfamiliar words

Students sometimes blame unfamiliar words for their reading difficulties. In this section we will study strategies for dealing with these words.

Task 9 (Individual)

Study this list of 'difficult words' from a passage. In not more than three minutes, try to find the meaning of any of these words which are unfamiliar to you.

intricate result
hitherto rush
embarking

Task 10 (Individual)

Now read the passage in which a student counsellor describes study difficulties. Answer these questions:

1. What is the most common complaint of students?
2. Why do some postgraduates experience this problem?

> When I began the work, I expected most of my time to be spent helping students with fairly complex cognitive difficulties with their efforts to grasp higher-order concepts or to reproduce intricate

patterns of argument. It surprised me to discover that the most common 'complaint' of students of all ages, levels of study and disciplines, is difficulty in organising and timetabling their work. Many students identify this as a problem fairly soon after embarking on a first year at university, but many do not until after examinations at the end of their first term. Yet others come to discuss methods of organising themselves in something of a rush before resit exams; and I find now that an increasing number of highly successful graduates come with the same concern soon after embarking on a higher degree course that is less structured than anything they have hitherto experienced.

Main, A.N. (1980) *Encouraging Effective Learning*, p. 16 (Edinburgh: Scottish Academic Press).

It has been estimated that you will meet 80,000 to 100,000 different words in your textbooks in a typical course. It is impossible to know the meaning of all of these words. The first decision to make when faced with an unfamiliar word is '*Do I need to know its meaning?*' You can only answer this question if you have a clear purpose in your reading. Which of the words listed in Task 9 did you need to know the meaning of to answer the questions?

Task 11 (Individual)

In this passage, some words have been missed out to represent unfamiliar words. These are shown by the letters (a) to (e). Word (e) occurs twice. Which of these missing words do you need in order to answer these questions briefly? Write the appropriate letters, (a) to (e), in the table below to show which missing words you need.

1. According to Sexton, how are successful and unsuccessful students similar?
2. What differences does Sexton note between successful and unsuccessful students?
3. How do Borrow's ideas differ from those of Sexton?
4. Whose views does Small support, Sexton or Borrow?

Question	*Missing words needed*
1.	
2.	
3.	
4.	

There is a certain amount of *(a)* .... opinion about the characteristics of the successful student. Sexton (1965), reviewing twenty-five years of research into failure, reports that successful and unsuccessful students are likely to *(b)* .... 'bad' study habits with equal frequency. She reports that many investigations find that successful students spend more time in study, and tend to *(c)* .... the amount of study they do to the amount they think is needed for success in

> different subjects. Borrow (1946) believes that techniques, skills, *(d)* .... and attitudes are more important than the number of hours; his findings are that superior students are characterised by a more *(e)* .... schedule. Small (1966) shows a positive and highly significant relationship between academic success and adherence to a *(e)* .... method of study.
>
> Main, A.N. op. cit., p. 16.

Task 12 (Individual, then groups)

Go back to the table in Task 11. If you listed any 'Missing words needed', try to divide the words into two groups:

1. exact meaning needed
2. approximate meaning needed

The second decision to make when faced with an unfamiliar word is '*Do I need to know its exact meaning or its approximate meaning?*'

If you need to know the exact meaning of a word, what strategies can you use? Make a list of ideas in your group. Then compare your suggestions with those given in the *Key*.

Most of the time when you read, an approximate meaning is sufficient. In this book we will examine strategies for finding approximate meaning. The first step in finding the approximate meaning of an unfamiliar word is to identify what kind of word it is – noun, verb, adjective, etc. This limits the range of possible meanings. You can identify what kind of word it is by noting its position in the sentence and, where these exist, any clues in the form of the word, for example verb endings. Your knowledge of grammar will help you here.

Task 13 (Individual, then groups)

In this text, try to identify which kind of word each blank represents. Some clues in the form of the word are given.

Discuss your answers in your group.

> Some students have to do all their studying in libraries because their home is not suitable. However, libraries tend to become overcrowded. It is an advantage to have a room of your own where you can study. To convert a room into a study, remember the following points:
>
> 1. If you can choose which room to study in, choose one which is not near the *(a)* ...., kitchen, or the front door.
> 2. If you can, use the room for study only. If you live in a bed-sitting room and *(b)* .... to use it for other purposes such as sleeping or eating, it is sometimes difficult to study there. If the room has a bed, you may be *(c)* ....ed to study lying down. This is rarely *(d)* ....ful. It is also much more difficult to make sure *(e)* ....ic chores do not encroach on your study time.
> 3. Is the lighting adequate? Is there enough *(f)* ....ation? Is the temperature right? Is there *(g)* ....ly to be much noise or interruption?

4. Get some basic furniture. You *(h)* .... have a large table or desk, a desk lamp and a small bookcase for reference books. It is also useful to have some sort of *(i)* ....ing system for your folders.

5. Put a large notice board on one of the walls if you can. Pin on it:
   the regulations
   the syllabuses
   the list of lectures
   the year's *(j)* ....

6. If you are studying at the Open University, and do not live near a Study Centre, you may also want to buy a radio and perhaps buy or rent a television set as well.

7. Think carefully *(k)* .... the arrangement of the furniture. For example, place the desk near the window to take advantage of daylight.

8. Those who live with their families have a *(l)* ....ial problem, as not all the members of the family may understand that there are several hours during the day in which you should not be interrupted. You must explain how important your study is.

9. Tell your friends which evenings you will be studying so that they do not visit your home and *(m)* .... you.

Parsons, C. (1976) *How to Study Effectively*, pp. 22–3 (London: Arrow Books Ltd).

APPLICATION

Task 14 (Individual)

Study this extract from the summary of a chapter called 'Meet your memory', from a guide for students on how to improve memory. Make a list of the main questions this chapter deals with.

There is no such thing as a memory in the sense of some *thing* that can be
seen, touched, or weighed. Memory is an abstraction referring to a set of
1 skills rather than to an object. Neither is there a single standard for judging a
good or poor memory. There are a number of different ways in which a person may have a "good" memory.

Memory is generally viewed as consisting of three stages: (1) acquisition
refers to learning the material; (2) storage refers to keeping the material in
the brain until it is needed; and (3) retrieval refers to getting the material
back out when it is needed. These three stages may be viewed as the 3 R's of
2 Remembering: Recording, Retaining, and Retrieving. Retrieving is where
most problems come. We cannot do much about retrieval directly; but since
retrieval is a function of recording, we can improve it by improving our
methods of recording.

Memory consists of at least two different processes: short-term memory
and long-term memory. Short-term memory has a limited capacity and a
3 rapid forgetting rate. Its capacity can be increased by chunking, or grouping
separate bits of information into larger chunks. Long-term memory has a

LIVERPOOL
JOHN MOORES UNIVERSITY
AVRIL ROBARTS LRC
TEL 0151 231 4022

virtually unlimited capacity. Short-term memory and long-term memory also differ in several other ways.

One measure of memory is recall, which requires you to produce information by searching the memory for it. In aided recall, you are given cues to help you produce the information. In free-recall learning you recall the material in any order; in serial learning you recall it in the order it was presented; and in paired-associate learning you learn pairs of words so that when the first word is given you can recall the second word. A second measure of
4 memory is recognition, in which you do not have to produce the information from memory, but must be able to identify it when it is presented to you. In a third measure of memory, relearning, the difference between how long it took to learn the material the first time and how long it takes to learn it again indicates how much you remember. Relearning is generally a more sensitive measure of memory than is recognition, in the sense of showing retention where recognition does not; recognition is generally a more sensitive measure than recall.

Some material may be remembered in visual form (pictures), and other material may be remembered in verbal form (words). Some research evidence indicates that there are two different memory processes for these two
5 kinds of material. Pictures may be processed differently from words, and concrete words high in imagery may be processed differently from abstract words low in imagery. Visual images are easier to remember than words alone, leading some researchers to suggest that we should try to use visual images as much as possible in memory.

There are several explanations of why we forget. Passive-decay theory says that learning causes a physical "trace" in the brain that decays with time. Repression theory says that we purposely push unpleasant or unacceptable memories into our unconscious mind. Systematic-distortion theory says that our memories may be distorted by our values and interests, to be consistent
6 with how we want the memories to be or how we think they should be. Interference theory says that forgetting is due to interference by other learning. Retrieval failure theory says that forgetting is due to problems in retrieving the information, and that we can remember almost anything if given the right cues. The last two of these explanations are the ones of most interest in this book.

Higbee, K.L. (1977) *Your Memory, How it Works and How to Improve it*, pp. 34–6 (Englewood Cliffs, New Jersey: Prentice-Hall, Inc.).

Task 15 (Individual)

Study this illustration from the same chapter. Write three questions answered by this illustration.

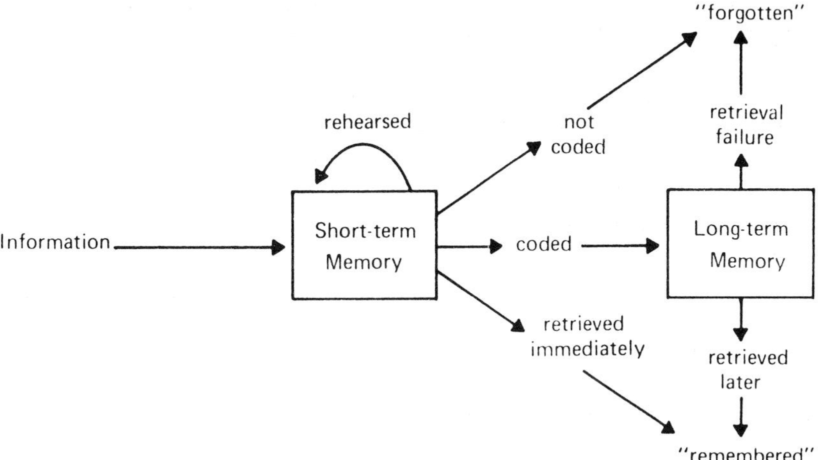

Higbee, K.L. op. cit., p. 18.

Which paragraph in the summary refers to the information contained in the illustration?

Task 16 (Individual)

Compare your list of questions from Task 14 with these section headings and subsection headings for this chapter. Note that the section headings are in the form of questions. How similar are they to your questions?

Meet your memory
WHAT ARE THE STAGES OF MEMORY?
WHAT ARE SHORT-TERM AND LONG-TERM MEMORY?
Short-term memory
Long-term memory
HOW CAN WE MEASURE MEMORY?
Recall
Recognition
Relearning
HOW DO WE REMEMBER PICTURES VERSUS WORDS?
WHY DO WE FORGET?
Passive decay
Repression
Systematic distortion
Interference

PART 2 KNOWING WHAT'S IMPORTANT

Unit 3 The spirit of enquiry

Having a spirit of enquiry is an important part of being a student. The aim of study is to increase our personal understanding of the world. The purpose of research is to add to the sum of human knowledge. In this unit you will read about methods of enquiry to increase our own understanding and advance the frontiers of knowledge. The topics covered in this unit are: designing experiments, problem solving, carrying out surveys and making questionnaires.

You will not only read about methods of enquiry, you will also take part in an experiment to find out how to read more effectively.

This unit aims to develop the reading skills required for:

1. surveying a text
2. understanding how facts and ideas are connected
3. understanding unfamiliar words from their immediate context

TO MAKE YOU THINK

Task 1 (Pairs)

Look at this statement.

Male birds sing to attract female birds.

Working with your partner, try to devise an experiment to investigate this claim. Note briefly the method you would use.

Task 2 (Pairs)

Study this introduction to a report of an experiment to investigate why male birds sing. The text contains some specialist vocabulary. Use the strategies you studied in Unit 2 to decide if you need to know the meaning of any of these words. Find out the meaning only of words you consider important.

> Male passerine birds are noted for their singing. Considerable study has been made of the frequency, duration and even regional variation in their song (Swales et al, 1984). Most ornithologists have taken it for granted that they sing to attract females. But no one has produced any evidence to support this assumption. Our study focussed on the pied flycatcher (Ficedula hypoleuca) and the collared flycatcher (Ficedula albicollis). It involved setting up nesting-box traps in a known nesting site near Uppsala, Sweden.

Does this text give you any new ideas about how to conduct your experiment? Think again about your method. Note any changes.

Task 3 (Individual, then groups)

We will study another text which may help you with the design of your experiment. The title is 'Conducting Biological Experiments'. Before you read, try to predict some of the words and ideas which may come into the text. Note them down.

Share your ideas with the others in your group.

Task 4 (Class)

Here are some of the words which appear in the text. Are any the same as the ones you wrote down in Task 3? Try to explain what the connection is between the title and each of the words surrounding it. In what order would you expect to find these words? Share your ideas with the others in your class.

hypothesis	*confirmed*	*conclude*
significant	CONDUCTING BIOLOGICAL EXPERIMENTS	*results*
investigation	*suggest*	*predict*

Task 5 (Individual, then pairs)

As you read this text, try to predict how it will continue at each numbered point. Test your prediction by selecting what you consider the most logical of the alternatives given. You will probably find when you read on that you have not always chosen correctly. If this happens, go back and read the section again. Have you failed to make the correct guess because the text is not clear or because you have missed some clues which could have helped you?

When you have completed this task, compare your answers with your neighbour.

Conducting biological experiments

A hypothesis stands or falls on the experiments that are carried out to test it. It is therefore essential to

1. a) make a sensible hypothesis.
   b) do the right experiment in the right way.

The predictions made from the hypothesis should tell the investigator exactly what experiments need to be done. This might seem obvious, but it is surprising how often a student, having formulated a very sensible hypothesis, goes on to

2. a) devise experiments which do not test it at all.
   b) make highly inaccurate predictions.

Often a single crucial experiment is enough to settle the matter. Here is an example.

On the basis that all cells have one, we conclude that the nucleus is

3. a) essential for life.
   b) the central part of cells.

From this we predict that a cell without a nucleus will die. The experimental test is obvious: assuming that it is technically feasible, we must

4. a) examine as many cells as possible.
   b) remove the nucleus from a cell and see what happens.

Enucleation of cells is possible, at any rate with a large cell like *Amoeba*. The nucleus is carefully sucked out with a very fine pipette. It is found, as predicted, that

5. a) the cell dies.
   b) the cell survives.

But can we be certain that it is the absence of the nucleus which causes death, and not

6. a) factors in the environment?
   b) the damage inflicted on the cell during the operation?

To find the answer to this we must set up a control: a second *Amoeba* has its nucleus removed in exactly the same way, and then immediately

7. a) destroyed.
   b) put back again.

The same amount of damage is done to the cell but it is not permanently deprived of its nucleus. Apart from this the two *Amoebae* must be

8. a) treated quite differently.
   b) kept in exactly the same conditions.

The control *Amoebae* do in fact survive, suggesting (proving?) that it is

9. a) the absence of the nucleus
   b) the damage done in removing the nucleus

which causes death. Setting up appropriate controls is an essential part of any investigation. It provides a standard with which the experimental situation can be compared.

One further point before we leave this topic. It is not sufficient to do the experiment on only one pair of *Amoebae*, even though

10. a) they may give the expected results.
    b) this is very time-consuming.

The experiment must be repeated many times, and consistent results obtained, before this prediction can be regarded as confirmed. The quickest way of doing this in the case described above is to set up a group of enucleated *Amoebae*, perhaps 50 in all (the experimental group). At the same time we prepare a control group of non-enucleated specimens. If we are lucky it may turn out that all the individuals in the experimental group die, whereas

11. a) all those in the control group survive.
    b) all those in the control group die.

But in biological experiments it often turns out that only a proportion of the tests

12. a) prove anything.
    b) give the expected results.

In such cases it may be necessary to repeat the experiment over and over again, and subject the results to statistical analysis, to establish whether the results are significant or merely the result of chance.

Roberts, M.B.V. (1986) *Biology: A Functional Approach*, 4th edition, pp. 5–6 (Walton-on-Thames: Thomas Nelson and Sons Ltd).

Task 6 (Pairs)

With your partner, think again about the design of your experiment in Task 1. Can you improve it further?

When you have completed your discussion, read the brief report in the *Key*. Note any differences between your experiment and the one described.

READING AND INTERACTION

Surveying a text

'Surveying' a text means reading to obtain a general idea of its contents. Surveying depends on good sampling. In your mother tongue you don't read a text word by word. You read a little – take a sample – and predict what will come next. The sample provides clues as to how the text will continue. Then you take another sample and adjust your prediction. Each time, the sample provides clues as to how the text will continue.

Reading for the general idea depends on good sampling – knowing where to look, knowing which parts of the text can help us most. Because we don't read everything when we read for the general idea, this kind of reading also depends on good prediction skills.

As you become a more experienced reader, you will sample more effectively. Consequently your predictions will become more accurate. In the tasks that follow we will try to find out what parts of a text can provide the best samples.

Task 7 (Individual)

Study this list of questions about a text. The text describes an experiment in problem solving. When you can answer all of the questions correctly, you will have a general idea of the text.

1. What is functional fixity?
2. What task were the groups asked to do?
3. What was the single difference between the groups?
4. What were the results?
5. What conclusion can we make from these results?
6. What was the effect of the extra objects?

We are going to look at different samples of the text to find out which samples help us most to get a general idea of the text.

→

Now study Sample 1. Which questions does it help you to answer? Think about this before you read on.

Sample 1 (Title and illustrations)

FUNCTIONAL FIXITY: A BARRIER TO CREATIVE PROBLEM SOLVING

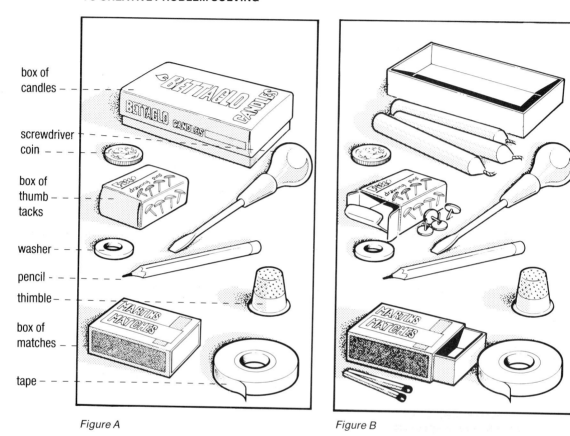

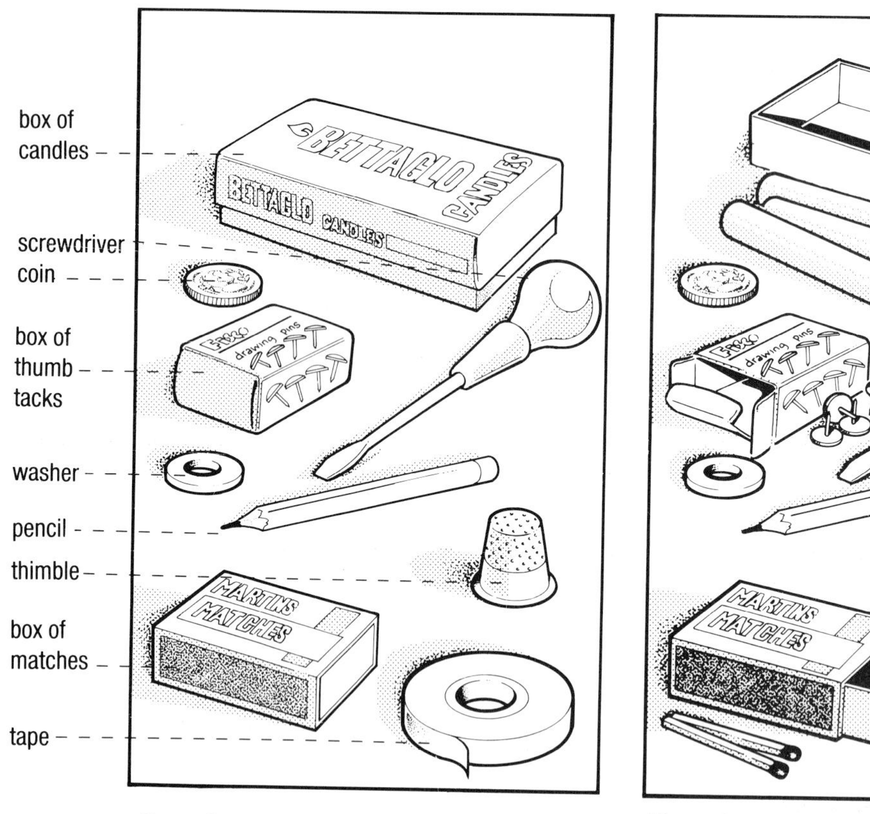

Figure A

Figure B

Now study Sample 2. Does it help you to answer more of the questions? Does it help you to give better answers to some of the questions?

Sample 2 (First sentence of each paragraph added)

FUNCTIONAL FIXITY: A BARRIER TO CREATIVE PROBLEM SOLVING

The German psychologist Karl Duncker first proposed the concept of functional fixity about 1930, and he illustrated it with a few simple experiments.

The task: Mount three candles vertically on a soft wooden screen, using any object on the table.

For one group (twenty-nine college students), the candles, matches, and tacks were placed *in* the

three boxes before they were presented to the subjects (Figure A).

Of the first group, only twelve of the subjects (or 41 percent) were able to solve the problem: apparently the remaining subjects in this group could not perceive the boxes with the meaning of platform or shelf.

These results give striking evidence that functional fixity may be an important barrier in creative problem solving.

R. E. ADAMSON. Functional fixedness as related to problem-solving, *Journal of Experimental Psychology*, 1952, 44, 288–291.

Give as full an answer to each question as you can *before* you read on.

Now study Sample 3. Does it help you to answer more of the questions? Does it help you to give better answers to some of the questions? Try to draw the solution to the problem the subjects were set.

Sample 3 (First and last paragraphs added)

FUNCTIONAL FIXITY: A BARRIER TO CREATIVE PROBLEM SOLVING

The German psychologist Karl Duncker first proposed the concept of functional fixity about 1930, and he illustrated it with a few simple experiments. Because these experiments were done with so few subjects, several American psychologists repeated them, and they obtained results similar to Duncker's. R. E. Adamson at Stanford University did one such experiment.

The task: Mount three candles vertically on a soft wooden screen, using any object on the table.

For one group (twenty-nine college students), the candles, matches, and tacks were placed *in* the

three boxes before they were presented to the subjects (Figure A).

Of the first group, only twelve of the subjects (or 41 percent) were able to solve the problem: apparently the remaining subjects in this group could not perceive the boxes with the meaning of platform or shelf.

These results give striking evidence that functional fixity may be an important barrier in creative problem solving. Note also the mental dazzle operating here, as a result of the useless, hence distracting, extra objects.

R. E. ADAMSON. Functional fixedness as related to problem-solving, *Journal of Experimental Psychology*, 1952, 44, 288–291.

Task 8 (Groups)

Compare your answers and your drawings with the others in your group. Discuss any differences. Then check the accuracy of your answers and your drawings with the complete text in the *Key*.

Which samples of the text gave you the most help with the questions? Which questions could not be answered fully? Do you think that sampling in this way could be useful for all texts?

TEXT EXPLORATION

Discourse study: Linking words

While sampling will help us to obtain a general idea of a text, we need to know how the facts and ideas which compose the text are linked to understand the meaning of the text in detail. We will study here how writers link facts and ideas.

Task 9 (Individual, then pairs)

Complete these sentences about questionnaires and interviews. Compare your completed sentences with your partner.

1. Questionnaires are cheaper than interviews because . . .
2. Interviews are expensive, whereas . . .
3. People often fill in questionnaires without much thought. As a result, . . .
4. Postal questionnaires have a poor response rate; i.e. . . .

Task 10 (Individual)

Here is another example for you to try. This time try to predict how the text will continue at each numbered point.

When making a questionnaire, avoid imprecise terms like 'occasionally' and 'sometimes' since
1. a) people understand such words in different ways.
   b) you should use shorter words.

Consequently, if your questionnaire includes such terms,
2. a) it will be very lengthy.
   b) it will not be reliable.

In other words,
3. a) it will not provide consistent results.
   b) it will be very expensive to produce.

For example, a teenager may answer that she listens to pop music 'occasionally' but her mother may respond that she listens
4. a) 'very often'.
   b) about three hours a week.

Authors often use linking words and phrases to mark the connections between the ideas in their writing. Knowing these words will help you both to understand how the ideas in a text are connected and also to make more accurate predictions as you read. Study these examples and try to add further linking words and phrases to the table.

Idea	*Marked by these linking words and phrases*
Reason	because, since
Contrast	whereas, but
Conclusion	consequently, as a result
Rephrasing	i.e., in other words
Example	for example, for instance
Addition	furthermore, in addition

Task 11 (Individual)

Select the correct linking word or phrase from the two alternatives given.

Reliability and validity

Reliability and validity are key concepts in any form of enquiry. Reliability is a measure of consistency. *Furthermore / For example*, if a clock is sometimes fast and sometimes slow, it is unreliable. If a questionnaire produces different results for the same group of people each time it is used, then the questionnaire is unreliable.

Validity is a measure of truth. It is possible for a questionnaire to be highly reliable yet invalid, like a clock which is always ten minutes slow. *In contrast / In other words*, a clock which is always right provides a valid and reliable measure of time. Similarly, a questionnaire which really measures what it claims to measure is a valid questionnaire. We can assess how valid our questionnaire is by comparing its results with an independent measure. *In addition / For instance*, if we ask people how often they visit their local theatre and then check the results against ticket sales, we will know how valid our questionnaire is. *However / Because* independent measures are themselves often unreliable and of low validity. *Furthermore / Consequently*, in many cases there are no independent measures. *In other words / However*, a 'true' answer does not exist.

LIVERPOOL
JOHN MOORES UNIVERSITY
AVRIL ROBARTS LRC
TEL. 0151 231 4022

Word study: Using immediate context

Task 12 (Individual)

In Unit 2 we studied the first steps in finding out the approximate meaning of unfamiliar words – identifying the kind of word, the part of speech as a means of limiting the range of meaning. This text contains some words in **bold** type which may be unfamiliar to you. Identify the part of speech of each word. Then try to guess the meaning of each word as it is used in the text. Do not use a dictionary at this stage. The text discusses some of the problems of using questionnaires rather than interviews.

Word	*Part of speech*	*Meaning*
drawbacks		
spontaneous		
ambiguity		
independent		

> Questionnaires have certain obvious advantages, but they also have **drawbacks**. **Spontaneous** answers cannot be distinguished from thought-out answers. Questions can be misunderstood because it is difficult to avoid **ambiguity** except in the most simple questions. Different answers cannot be treated as **independent** since the subject can see all the questions before answering any one of them.

The second step in working out the meaning of an unfamiliar word is to examine the immediate context of the word – the sentence in which it appears. Often the sentence contains enough clues to help you to get an approximate meaning of the word. Linking words can help. Study these examples:

1. Questionnaires have certain obvious advantages,
   but (=expect a contrast)
   they also have **drawbacks**.

   The contrast is between 'advantages' and 'drawbacks'. Hence we can work out that 'drawbacks' means 'disadvantages'.

Sometimes words which are opposites are contrasted in a sentence. If you know the meaning of one of these words, you can find out the meaning of the other. For example:

2. **Spontaneous** answers cannot be
   distinguished from (=expect an opposite)
   thought-out answers.

   Hence we can work out that a spontaneous answer is one which is not thought-out. In other words, 'spontaneous' means 'without thinking'.

Check in your dictionary for a more accurate definition.

There are many other immediate context clues which help the experienced reader deal with unfamiliar words. Some of these are practised in Task 13.

Task 13 (Individual, then pairs)

Study these sentences which list some of the advantages and disadvantages of using questionnaires and interviews. Try to guess the meaning of each of the words in **bold** type. Underline the clues in the sentence which help you to work out the meaning. When you have finished, compare ideas with your neighbour. Then check the accuracy of your guesses using a dictionary.

1. The interview is a **flexible** tool which can be altered to suit its role in the study.
2. Replies can be more **candid** since respondents do not have to commit themselves in writing.
3. The interviewer can distinguish between a genuine and an **insincere** response.
4. Interviewers can control the sequence of items; hence the respondent cannot look ahead and **anticipate** the trend of the enquiries.
5. The problem of taking full notes of a conversation during an interview is usually solved by **restricting** writing to marks or numbers.
6. Interviewers may give an **inkling** of their own opinion or expectations by their tone of voice, the way in which they read the questions, or simply by their appearance, dress and accent.
7. Questionnaires can be **anonymous** – but not if identification is required for follow-up study.
8. Respondents fill in their own answers and so cannot be **misheard**.

APPLICATION

In this section we will practise sampling and prediction skills. Each of the texts is a short report about experiments and investigations.

Task 14 (Individual)

Study this list of titles. Try to predict what each text will be about. You may use a dictionary.

1. Rapid revolution is the answer
2. Small and mighty fibres
3. Healthy advice for economy class high-flyers
4. The origin of arthritis

Task 15 (Individual)

These illustrations belong to two of the texts. Match the illustrations to the titles. Refine your predictions for these two texts.

Figure 1

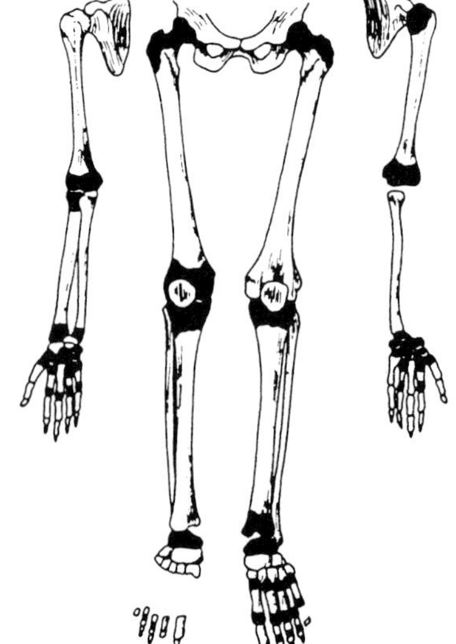

Figure 2

Task 16 (Individual)

Study the complete texts in the *Key*. Sample the parts which you think will help you most to predict the main points. Do not spend more than one minute on any one text.

Task 17 (Individual)

Write down your predictions of the main points of each text without looking back at the text. Then read each text at your own speed to check your predictions.

Unit 4 The developing world

Whether we live in the developed world or the developing world, the issues which confront the three quarters of the world's population who inhabit the developing world are important to all of us. The texts in this unit deal with some of these issues.

This unit aims to develop the reading skills required for:
1. identifying important points
2. understanding text structure

TO MAKE YOU THINK

Task 1 (Individual, then groups)

Make a list of five countries which you think belong to the developing world. Why do you think they should be classified in this way? What issues are of particular importance to such countries? Discuss your answers with your group and make a list of the important issues.

Task 2 (Individual)

Study this contents page from a publication which deals with developing world issues. Which headings will cover the issues you have listed as important to developing countries? Match your list with the contents headings.

Contents **i**

Agriculture and rural planning	217
Natural resources	247
Economic development	259
Demography, population and migration	278
Health, food and nutrition	284
Social policy, planning and social services	291
Urbanisation and urban planning	298
Regional and spatial planning	302
Women and minorities	304
Education and training	310
Labour and management	314

International relations, conflict, cooperation and aid	315
Trade	320
Transport and communications	323
Technology	326
Energy	328
Concepts and methodology	329
Culture and society	331
Institutional framework and administration	334
Politics	337
Regional Index	342

Amos, M. (ed.) (1990) *International Development Abstracts*, Contents page, 3, (Barking: Elsevier Science Publishers Ltd).

Task 3 (Individual, then groups)

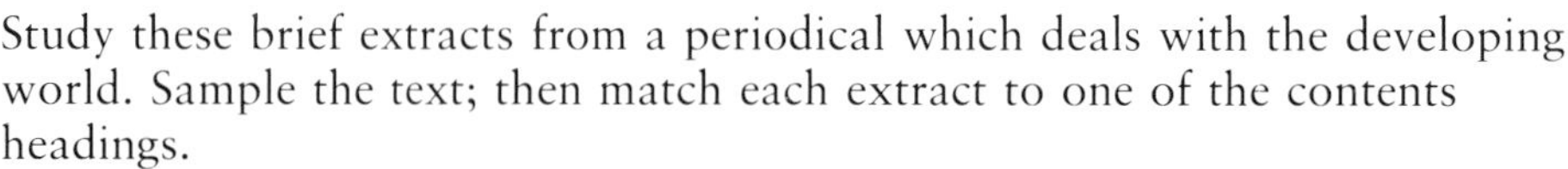

Study these brief extracts from a periodical which deals with the developing world. Sample the text; then match each extract to one of the contents headings.

a)

THE QUANTITY KEY

80% of disease in developing countries is related to poor drinking water and sanitation. Water quantity is even more important than quality when it comes to health – because a lot of water is needed to keep the body and household clean. The key to increasing the water consumption of the poor is giving them easier access to a supply. Until their distance from a source is reduced to less than five minutes' walk, water consumption does not rise significantly.[8]

HOUSEHOLD WATER CONSUMPTION [2]

Households with dishwashers, washing machines, and sprinklers: 1,000 litres a head per day

Households with a piped supply and taps: 100-350 litres a head per day

Households using a public hydrant in the street: 20-70 litres a head per day

Households depending on a stream or handpump several miles distant: 2-5 litres a head per day

b)

ROLLERCOASTER GONE WILD

The prices of the raw materials on which Third World economies depend have been in steady decline. In 1987 they reached their lowest level for 50 years.

Index (1979 - 81 = 100)

150, 125, 100, 75, 50

Metals and minerals·······

Nonfuel primary commodities———

Real commodity prices 1970-88[5]

1970, 1975, 1980, 1985, 1988

c)

THE LONGEST-LIVED ...

Life expectancy in years[8]

	1975	1987	% increase
1. Japan	73	78	7
2. Canada	72	77	7
2. Holland	74	77	4
2. Norway	75	77	3
2. Spain	72	77	7
2. Sweden	73	77	5
2. Switzerland	72	77	7
8. Australia	72	76	6
8. UK	72	76	6
8. US	71	76	7[9]

AND THE SHORTEST

Life expectancy in years[10]

	1975	1987	% increase
1. Afghanistan	35	42	20
1. Ethiopia	38	42	10
1. Sierra Leone	44	42	-5
4. Guinea	41	43	5
5. Angola	39	45	15
5. Mali	38	45	18
5. Niger	39	45	15
8. Cent Afr Rep	41	46	12
8. Chad	39	46	18
8. Somalia	41	46	12

d)

HOW IT CHANGES

Slowly, all too slowly, once-poor countries have been increasing their share of world trade in manufactures. Not all of the increase comes from the classic 'Newly Industrializing Countries' of South Korea, Taiwan, Hong Kong and Singapore. Mexico and Brazil have been industrializing for many years, and are being joined by Thailand, Malaysia, Morocco, Mauritius and many others. India, Pakistan and China are beginning to move. Meanwhile the market shares of both Europe and the US are eroding.

Percentage shares of world manufacturing trade[2]

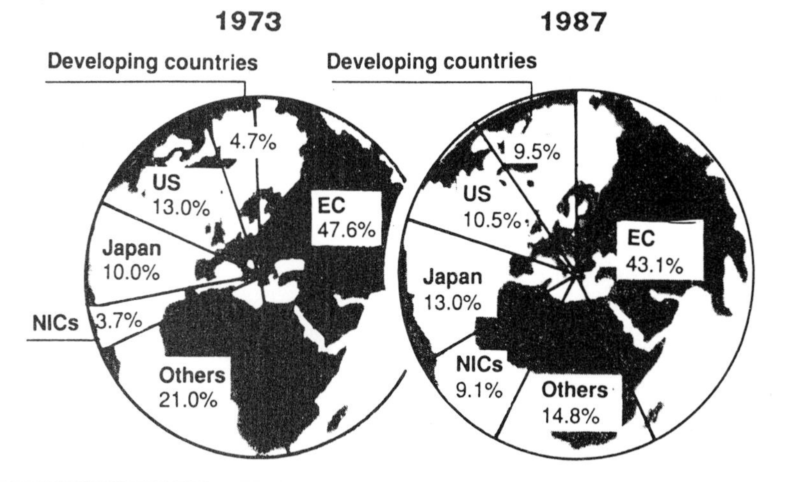

e)

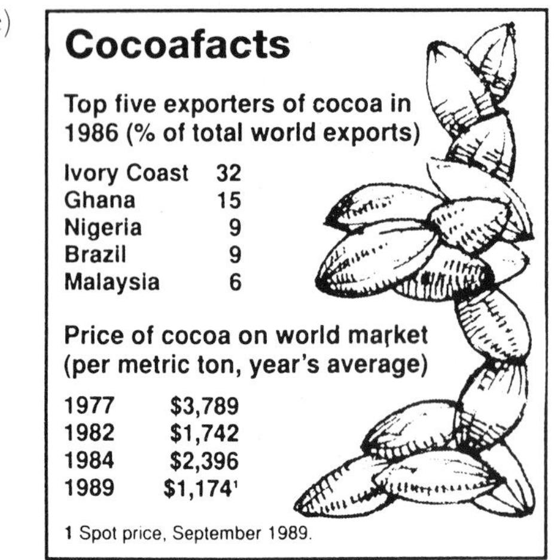

Cocoafacts

Top five exporters of cocoa in 1986 (% of total world exports)

Ivory Coast	32
Ghana	15
Nigeria	9
Brazil	9
Malaysia	6

Price of cocoa on world market (per metric ton, year's average)

1977	\$3,789
1982	\$1,742
1984	\$2,396
1989	\$1,174[1]

1 Spot price, September 1989.

New Internationalist Publications, Oxford
a) May 1990, p. 17
b) Oct. 1989, p. 16
c) Oct. 1989, p. 17
d) Feb. 1990, p. 16
e) Feb. 1990, p. 15
f) June 1989, p. 48

f)

WOMEN

The Literacy Gap

There are more illiterate women than men in every region of the world. An illiterate is defined by UNESCO as a person 'who cannot with understanding both read and write a short simple statement of his/her everyday life'. And the literacy gap between the sexes, which grows in proportion to the rate of illiteracy, is most pronounced in Africa followed by Asia, Latin America and finally, the developed countries.

From UNESCO Sources, no 2, March 1989.

Female/male illiteracy rates for over 15 year-olds in the world. (1985)

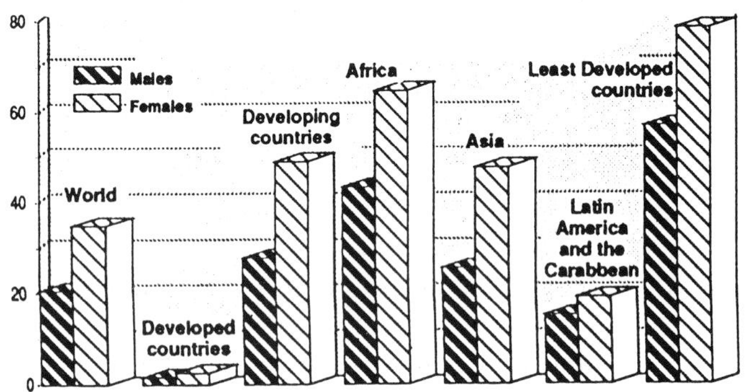

Task 4 (Individual, then pairs)

Underline what you think are the most important points in this text. Compare your choices with your partner.

Discuss how you made your selection of points.

Too many mouths

One of the most important problems facing developing countries today is the rapid increase in population. In the last 25 years, the population of the world has doubled. As the developing world has a population growth rate which is twice that of the developed world, most of that population increase has taken place in the poorer countries of the world. The main point to be made here is that more and more people are concentrated in those countries which are least able to provide a living for them.

What is responsible for this population rise is not an increase in fertility, but a sharp decline in the death rate in developing countries. In the absence of birth control, the maximum birth rate is around 4%. For a population to remain static in these circumstances, the death rate would have to be the same. Improving food supplies can reduce the death rate to 3%. Better public health and medical care can cut the death rate by a further 2%. The resultant population growth of 3% will double the population every 25 years.

The main reason for the reduction in the death rate in the developing world has been improved public health measures. For example, in Sri Lanka the death rate was halted over ten years by spraying the mosquitoes which carry malaria. Why is it so easy to cut the death rate in this way and yet so hard to reduce the birth rate? One answer is that public health measures can be very cheap. Anti-malarial spraying is inexpensive. But this is not the important point. For birth control programmes to be successful, a change in attitude is required, whereas death control can be achieved autonomously. In other words, the death rate can be cut without anything else changing.

This text draws on ideas from *Worlds Apart: The economic gulf between nations*, Peter Donaldson, BBC Publications, London, 1971.

READING AND INTERACTION

Reading for important points

In Unit 3 we studied how to survey a text to obtain a general idea of its contents. We found that good sampling – knowing *where* to look – and good prediction skills – making intelligent guesses based on these samples – were important when reading for the general idea.

Identifying what is important in a text depends on good sampling but it also depends on knowing *what* to look for – the clues which help us to identify the important points – and to separate them from the less important details.

Look again at this text from Task 4. Some of the words have been put in **bold** type.

> **The main reason for** the reduction in the death rate in the developing world has been improved public health measures. **For example**, in Sri Lanka the death rate was halved over ten years by spraying the mosquitoes which carry malaria. **Why** is it so easy to cut the death rate in this way and yet so hard to reduce the birth rate? **One answer** is that public health measures can be very cheap. Anti-malarial spraying is inexpensive. **But this is not the important point**. For birth control programmes to be successful, a change in attitude is required, whereas death control can be achieved autonomously. **In other words**, the death rate can be cut without anything else changing.

LIVERPOOL
JOHN MOORES UNIVERSITY
AVRIL ROBARTS LRC
TEL. 0151 231 4022

The words in **bold** type are signposts. They can help you to find the important parts of a text. They can also warn you that some things in the text are not so important. Let's examine some of the signposts writers use.

1. These phrases indicate an important point:
   The main / important point / conclusion / reason . . .
   The point to note here . . .
   Above all . . .

2. Sometimes we are told how many important points to expect. For example:
   There are three major reasons . . .

3. Important points may be highlighted using italics, bold type or capitals:
   An important requirement for development is **freedom from debt.**

4. 'But' and 'however' often indicate an important contrast, qualification or correction. For example:
   The rising birth rate is not due to increased fertility, **but** *to a sharp decline in the death rate.*

5. Asking a question in a text is a way of highlighting the answer which follows. For example:
   ***Why** is a piped water supply so important? Disease due to contaminated water is a common cause of death in childhood.*

6. A writer may repeat an important point to make sure it is understood. For example:
   Death control can be achieved autonomously. ***In other words,*** *the death rate can be cut without anything else changing.*

7. Conclusions are usually important. Look out for signposts such as:
   therefore *the result*
   in conclusion *we can conclude*
   one of the primary conclusions

8. Examples are usually less important, although a key example can help you to remember a main point. Examples are signposted by phrases such as:
   for example/instance *like*
   such as *these include*
   to illustrate *among these are*

   They may also be shown simply by punctuation. For example:
   The developing countries are dependent on cash crops – sugar, coffee, cacao, cotton.
   Precipitating factors are those which reduce the food supply (droughts, floods, wars, epidemics) . . .

Now read the text again. This time the meaning of each signpost has been added in brackets ( ).

> **The main reason for** (this is important) the reduction in the death rate in the developing world has been improved public health measures. **For example,** (this is only to illustrate) in Sri Lanka the death rate was halved over ten years by spraying the mosquitoes which carry malaria. **Why** (the answer to this question is important) is it so easy to cut the death rate in this way and yet so hard to reduce the birth rate? **One**

answer (this is only one answer – not the important one) is that public health measures can be very cheap. Anti-malarial spraying is inexpensive. **But this is not the important point** (now I'm going to tell you what the important point is). For birth control programmes to be successful, a change in attitude is required, whereas death control can be achieved autonomously. **In other words**, (this is so important I'll repeat it in simpler words) the death rate can be cut without anything else changing.

Task 5 (Individual)

The signposts in this text have been put in **bold** type. Put a tick (√) after those which indicate an important point and a cross (×) after those which indicate information which is less important.

Why is it so difficult to solve the unemployment problems of the developing world? [ ] There are **three main reasons.** [ ] **Firstly** [ ] there is the constant pressure of a rapidly rising population. This problem is made worse in cities by the drift of people from country areas to escape the poverty of rural life. **Then** [ ] there are problems of bad manpower planning. **For example,** [ ] a feature of unemployment in the developing world is the educated unemployed – the lawyers or arts graduates who have been trained at great expense for jobs which do not exist. **The point here** [ ] is that the manpower plan has not been matched to the production plan. **However, the major reason** [ ] for many countries failing to solve the unemployment problem has been their governments' preference for large-scale capital-intensive projects which use up scarce resources and have little impact on unemployment. **In fact,** [ ] by destroying local craft-based industry, such projects may even create further unemployment.

Task 6 (Individual)

Study this title and the opening sentence of a text.

THE FAMINE PROCESS

It is useful to identify three categories of cause of famines.

Make a list of all the reasons you can think of why famines sometimes occur in the developing world.

Task 7 (Individual)

Work in groups of three. Each choose a different text, 1, 2 or 3. Identify the main points and note them in the table on page 49.

Text 1

First, there are *long-term* causes of household income loss or income instability which increase the vulnerability of poor people. High among these in Africa is environmental degradation, affecting pastoralists in particular but also cultivators in arid and semi-arid areas. The Sahel, the Horn and western southern Africa are the areas where long-term factors have been increasing famine risk most. Social changes, particularly increased assetlessness among rural people, also increase famine risk. Among these are occupation of the best land by the rich and consequent loss of access by the poor and the breakdown of traditional social obligations to the poor.

Text 2

Second, there are *precipitating* factors, the events which dislodge the last food security of the poor, setting off the secondary events which worsen the situation – spiralling food prices, collapsing prices of rural assets (particularly livestock, because of lack of feed and the need to sell), calling in of debts, laying-off of employees, ultimately abandonment of the aged, the sick and the very young, and migration to towns. Precipitating factors include all those which actually reduce the food supply (drought, floods, war, epidemics) as well as those which it is feared will do so, and any which reduce the purchasing power of the poor.

Text 3

Third, there is *relief failure.* For famine to be precipitated, governmental famine-prevention administration must be inadequate, incompetent, or unable to operate. In Bengal 'administrative chaos' in the famine relief operation worsened the famine. In Bangladesh, improvement in famine relief administration during the 1970s greatly reduced famine in the early 1980s (see Ch. 5). Effective relief has prevented famine in Botswana and Gujarat state in India (see Ch. 5). Delays in relief have been a major factor in recent famines in Sudan and Ethiopia (see Ch. 3). The politics of famine relief (international and national) have played their part in worsening the Ethiopian and Mozambique famines through delaying the delivery of food aid (Tickner 1985: 91) while civil wars have severely hampered distribution.

Curtis, D., Hubbard, M. and Shepherd, A. (1988) *Preventing Famine, Policies and Prospects for Africa*, pp. 5, 6 abridged (London and New York: Routledge).

Causes of famine
Text 1
First category:
Causes: 1. 2.
Example of social changes:
Text 2
Second category:
Types of precipitating factors: 1. 2. 3.
Example of secondary events:
Text 3
Third category:
Example of relief failure:
Example of relief success:

Task 8 (Groups)

Find out from the others in your group the important points in their texts. Note them in the table. Make sure each section is complete.

When you have finished, read the remaining texts yourself. Do you agree with the choice of main points made by the others in your group? Discuss any differences in your group.

TEXT EXPLORATION

Discourse study: Signpost expressions

In the previous section, we studied how signpost expressions may help you to identify the important parts of a text. Writers may also use signpost expressions to indicate how the text is organised and to show when new topics are introduced.

Study these extracts from a text on desertification. Note the expressions which have been put in **bold** type.

> Deserts cover much of the world's surface. Each year over 100,000 km² of new desert is formed. This process is called desertification. **There are three major causes** of desertification: overcultivation, overgrazing and deforestation. Overcultivation and overgrazing are related causes and **I will discuss them first**. . . .
>
> **Let us consider now** deforestation which affects many parts of the developing world from the Himalayas to the Amazon basin. . . .
>
> **Can the process of desertification be halted?** A number of solutions have been attempted. One of the commonest is to plant belts of drought-resistant trees. . . .
>
> Given that the factors which lead to the misuse of land are unlikely to change in the next decade, **we may conclude that** the process of desertification will be slowed but not halted.

Study these signpost expressions.

1. Signposts which show the order in which topics will be covered:
   There are three major causes: . . . I will discuss them first.
2. Signposts which indicate a change of topic:
   Let us consider now . . .
   Having dealt with . . .
   Next . . .
   Lastly . . .

   Asking a question in a text can both indicate a change of topic and highlight the answer.
   Can the process of desertification *be halted?*
3. Signposts which indicate the end of a topic or the end of a text (this is a time to read carefully, as the main points are often made here):
   We may conclude that . . .
   In conclusion . . .

Grammar and meaning: Focussing structures

Writers use a number of structures to focus on part of a sentence to make it important. Look at these examples. The important parts are in **bold** type.

1. It is **environmental degradation** that causes famine in Africa.
2. What the World Health Organisation did was to **immunise everyone against smallpox.**
3. What lies behind the population explosion is **not a rise in fertility but a fall in the death rate.**

Task 9 (Individual)

Underline the important parts of these sentences.

1. What, above all, has reduced the death rate has been the transfer of medical technology.
2. It is because of bad manpower planning that there are so many educated unemployed.
3. What many governments wanted in the 1960s was large-scale capital-intensive projects.
4. It was spraying against malaria that halved the death rate.
5. What increases famine risk is social change.
6. It was rapid inflation that precipitated the Bengal famine of 1943.
7. It is in parts of Africa that long-term factors have increased famine risk most.
8. What we have to do is to remove the underlying causes of famine.

Grammar and meaning: Cause and effect links

Study these examples. What meaning link is shown by the words in **bold** type?

1. Better public health is **the reason for** reduction in the death rate.
2. Failure to prevent famine is **the greatest cause of** assetlessness among rural people.

How do these examples differ?

3. Famine may be **due to** environmental degradation.
4. The price of livestock collapses **because of** lack of feed.

Task 10 (Individual)

These sentences contain cause and effect links. Underline the cause or causes in each sentence.

1. Loss of purchasing power is one result of inflation.
2. Disasters may be due to the injustice of man or the injustice of nature.
3. Water shortage restricts the agricultural potential of some developing countries.
4. The pressure of population drives the poor to live in dangerous places.
5. Famine may result from drought, floods, war and epidemics.
6. Rising food prices worsen the situation.
7. Administrative incompetence leads to relief failure.
8. One of the main reasons for the unemployment problem is the pressure of a rapidly rising population.
9. Some capital-intensive projects may even create further unemployment.
10. Poverty leads to deforestation and desertification.

LIVERPOOL
JOHN MOORES UNIVERSITY
AVRIL ROBARTS LRC
TEL. 0151 231 4022

Word study: Word sets

One way to remember your growing vocabulary is to group the new words into sets according to their meaning. All of the words below share the idea of causing something to happen.

reduce	worsen	raise
aggravate	increase	double
create	impair	cut
halve	dislodge	lower
set off	restrict	

Task 11 (Individual, then pairs)

Group the verbs above into the following sets:

cause + START *cause* + MORE *cause* + LESS *cause* + HARM

APPLICATION

Task 12 (Individual)

Underline the main points in each paragraph. Then select the best summary from the three alternatives given after each paragraph.

> Disasters . . . are not entirely due to the injustice of nature: the injustice of man also plays its part. Poverty contributes both to the causation and impact of disaster. It is a major cause of deforestation and desertification, which aggravate floods and droughts. Poverty and the pressure of population drive the poor to live in increasingly dangerous places, like slums perched on steep slopes, or the flood- and cyclone-ridden islands of the Ganges delta in Bangladesh. Poor people can afford only flimsy houses of wood, mud and straw, liable to collapse in a heavy storm. Serious disasters appear to be increasing in frequency. A study by the University of Bradford found that the average number per year rose from five between 1919 and 1951, to eleven between 1951 and 1971, and over seventeen between 1968 and 1971. It seems unlikely that nature's inclemency is growing at this rate. The increase is probably due to the increasing disaster-proneness of the poor. But disasters of themselves accentuate poverty and make their victims more disaster-prone for the future.

1. a) Poverty makes the poor more disaster-prone, which results in more disasters and hence more poverty.
   b) The homes of poor people are easily destroyed in disasters.
   c) Poverty results in deforestation and desertification, which contribute to other disasters.

> All in all, the physical environment has not favoured the developing countries. The low productivity of the soil and of man has hampered growth and, along with the setbacks of variable rains and disasters, helped to prevent the emergence of a large and stable agricultural surplus. Such a surplus is the first requirement of development.

2. a) The soil in many developing countries is not very productive.
   b) Development requires a stable agricultural surplus.
   c) The environment makes it difficult to create the agricultural surplus required for development.

> There are some potential advantages in being closer to the sun. Given enough fertilisers and water, year-round sunshine can create an extraordinary agricultural potential, allowing as much as three crops a year. But water shortage restricts the areas where this is possible. As the oil runs out and solar power becomes more economical, the Third World will have greater supplies of endlessly renewable energy than the developed temperate zone countries.

3. a) Fertiliser and irrigation can increase the productivity of the developing world.
   b) Two potential advantages of ample sunshine are increased agricultural output and solar energy.
   c) The developed world has less solar energy potential than the developing world.

> But these prospects are as yet only hypothetical. Up to the present day, the hostile environment has been one of the key restraints in holding back economic development. It has raised the threshold of investment that the developing countries need to leap before they can industrialise. They need to invest more than western countries did at similar stages, in irrigation, flood control and erosion control for agriculture, and in human resources, to combat the effect of disease and heat on labour productivity.

4. a) Development has been held back because of the higher investment needed to overcome the effects of the environment.
   b) Irrigation and erosion control are very expensive for developing countries.
   c) Heat and disease reduce labour productivity.

> This investment hurdle was leapt in water control by the ancient empires of the Middle East, Asia and South America. It can be leapt again. Small-scale, labour-intensive technologies and basic health care involving the community can lower the cost of investment, while foreign aid and loans can help provide the necessary funds.

5. a) The ancient empires of the Middle East, Asia and South America solved the problem of irrigation.
   b) The investment problem can be overcome by focussing on less expensive technologies and community health care and by using loans and aid money.
   c) Foreign aid and loans can help development.

Harrison, P. (1982) *Inside the Third World*, 2nd edition, pp. 30, 31 (London: Penguin Books Ltd).

Unit 5 The natural world

In this unit we will study how to identify important points which are not clearly signposted. We will also study ways to help us remember the important points in a text.

The texts in this unit are concerned with the life sciences. This unit aims to develop the reading skills required for:
1. making inferences
2. note-taking

TO MAKE YOU THINK

Task 1 (Class)

What forms of wildlife are vulnerable in your own country? Why do you think this is so? Whose responsibility is it to preserve wildlife? How can this best be done?

Task 2 (Pairs)

Work in pairs, A and B.

Student A: Underline the main points in Text 1. Then compare your selection with your partner. Discuss how you made your choice.

Student B: Underline the main points in Text 2. Then compare your selection with your partner. Discuss how you made your choice.

Text 1

Most people would agree that the best way to conserve rare animals is to preserve their habitat. Even the best protected habitats are vulnerable. The poor, the hungry and those involved in civil war have no time for conservation. In the Sahel, a species of oryx has recently become extinct.

Many animals, especially predators, need a wide territory. If this is reduced, in the short term, drought, disease or war may cut their numbers. In the long term, inbreeding will cause extinction. Only one of the remaining wild dog populations in Africa is viable. For many animals, breeding in zoos is desirable. For larger animals, captive breeding is essential.

Text 2

Most people would agree that the best way to conserve rare animals is to preserve their habitat. But even the best protected habitats are vulnerable, because the poor, the hungry and those involved in civil war have no time for conservation. In the Sahel, for example, a combination of drought and civil war has wiped out a species of oryx.

Many animals, especially predators, need a wide territory. If this is reduced, in the short term, drought, disease or war may cut their numbers. In the long term, inbreeding will cause extinction. Only one of the remaining wild dog populations in Africa has sufficient protected territory to remain viable. It is clear that for many animals, breeding in zoos is desirable. For larger animals, such captive breeding is essential to maintain the species.

Now read each other's text. Which text is easier to understand? Why do you think this is so?

READING AND INTERACTION

Making inferences

Task 3 (Individual)

Look again at Text 1 opposite. Try to answer these questions:

1. Why are even the best protected habitats vulnerable?
2. Why has a species of oryx in the Sahel become extinct?
3. Why, in the long term, will animals whose territory is reduced become extinct?
4. What is captive breeding?
5. Why is captive breeding essential for larger animals?

Sometimes it can be difficult to understand a text because it contains few linking words and few signpost expressions. Text 1 is like this. In such situations, we have to make use of two kinds of information to make sense of what we read:

1. **Information from the text,** i.e. clues from the words, sentences and ideas which make up the text.
2. **Information from the reader,** i.e. clues from outside the text, from our own knowledge of the world.

To answer each of the questions in Task 3, we require both kinds of information. For example:

Question 1: *Why are even the best protected habitats vulnerable?*

Information required from the text:
The poor, the hungry and those involved in civil war have no time for conservation.

Information required from the reader:
In their fight to survive, such people may clear land for crops, overgraze their domestic animals and cut trees and shrubs for firewood.

Answer: *People who are poor, hungry or caught up in civil war may destroy the habitat of wild animals in their own struggle for survival.*

Combining information in this way is called 'making inferences'. It is one of the most important reading skills to develop.

Task 4 (Individual)

For each of questions 2 to 5 in Task 3, note down both the information you required from the text and the information you required from your own knowledge of the world.

Note-taking: Linear notes

Many of you will already have your own system for note-taking. If so, go through this section quickly to check for any ideas which are new to you.

When we take notes on a text, we have to do three things:

1. Recognise what's important
2. Reduce the important points to note form
3. Show how the important points are linked

We will deal here with 2 and 3.

Task 5 (Pairs, then groups)

One way to reduce important points to note form is to use symbols and abbreviations. Study this list of symbols and abbreviations. Work out what they mean. Compare your answers with others in your group. Can you add other examples of your own?

1. =
2. >
3. <
4. + + +
5. →
6. ←
7. ?
8. ??
9. re.
10. etc.
11. viz.
12. cf.
13. op. cit.
14. NB
15. ca
16. FAO
17. govt
18. hypoth.
19. prob.
20. imp.
21. ltd
22. std
23. v.
24. discussn

Task 6 (Individual)

Look again at examples 17–24 above. They illustrate how words can be abbreviated in English. What methods can you identify? For example:

Using first syllable *different* *diff.*

These symbols are commonly used in note-taking to show how important points are linked:

Idea	*Linking words*	*Symbols*
Reason	because, since	∵
Contrast	whereas, but	BUT
Conclusion	consequently, as a result	∴
Rephrasing	i.e., in other words	i.e.
Example	for example, for instance	e.g.
Addition	furthermore, in addition	&

Task 7 (Pairs)

You are going to read a text from *New Scientist*, the weekly review of science and technology. The title is:

'New Zealand's Marine Nature Reserves'

The author details are:

'Dr Bill Ballantine is a marine biologist at Leigh, New Zealand.'

Before you read further, discuss with your partner these questions:

1. What is a nature reserve?
2. What is a marine nature reserve?
3. Who might support marine nature reserves?
4. Who might oppose them?
5. What views might the author have about marine nature reserves?
6. What would you expect to find at Leigh, New Zealand?

Now read the first paragraph and reconsider your answer to Question 2.

FOR MANY years, all over the world, pieces of shore and shallow sea have been "reserved" for special purposes — harbours, shellfish farms, underwater cables, dredging for minerals, shipping channels, dumping sites, firing ranges and so on. Setting aside areas for no purpose at all but to leave them unused and unspoilt is a very new idea and has rarely been put into effect.

Task 8 (Groups)

The text goes on to discuss two approaches to marine reserves, one at Leigh and one at Poor Knights Islands. Work in groups, A and B.

Group A
Read Text 1 below, which is about the approach taken at Leigh. Try to agree on a set of notes that you feel summarises the main points. Your notes should have these sections:

Objectives
Criteria for selecting the reserve
Rules
Achievements
Disadvantages

Group B
Read Text 2 opposite, which is about the approach taken at Poor Knights Islands. Try to agree on a set of notes that you feel summarises the main points. Your notes should have the sections shown above.

Text 1

In the first approach, the main aim of the experiment is to learn the full effects of exploitation. This means a total ban on fishing, dredging and any other disturbance within the reserve. It is irrelevant whether damage is proven, who is carrying out the disturbance, or what their motivation is. The reserve must also be representative of a wide area, both biologically and in levels of exploitation. The next aim is to demonstrate the benefits, if any, that result from a natural unexploited state, and to maximise those benefits. To this end, the reserve should be easily accessible to the public and to researchers.

At Leigh the rules were simple and strict—no fishing, no removal of animals and no disturbance. The plan for management made no concessions to existing uses—commercial or recreational—if they conflicted with that policy. Even scientific experiments were permitted only if they caused disturbance within the limits of natural change. The site was reasonably typical of the open northeast coast in its biology, geology and fishing activity. Leigh's only special features were its accessibility: it is only an hour-and-a-half's drive from Auckland and close to the university's marine laboratory.

The Leigh reserve has proved remarkably successful in many ways. Despite predictions that a ban on fishing would mean there would be "nothing to do" at Leigh, more and more people visit the reserve. A recent survey showed that most visitors know that the area is a marine reserve before they come, yet they pass places where they could fish on their way, and they support the idea of more reserves with strict rules. Whether they are scuba divers, snorkellers or just beachcombers, visitors can see a greater variety of marine life, more abundantly and naturally than anywhere else.

The reserve has become a very active research site. The animals in the reserve live at more natural densities and distributions, and they behave more naturally. The site offers protection for experiments and recording equipment, and an assurance of continuity. There are detailed maps and plenty of background information.

The disadvantage of the approach adopted for the Leigh reserve was that people could no longer carry out many of their previous activities—but no one could provide them with any specific reasons for the ban. It took several years to convince large sections of the public that the experiment was worthwhile. The public then influenced the politicians, who instructed the administrators responsible for legislation. These officials were always less than enthusiastic about the radical approach. When they were spurred into action they much preferred the alternative method with limited aims.

Text 2

In the second approach to marine reserves, the main objective is to establish a working reserve without antagonising large numbers of existing users and all the protracted fuss that this can entail. The elimination of activities that are already known to have caused damage is a sufficient first step. This is why it is sensible to consult widely with those people who use the area, stressing that only those activities that are demonstrably damaging will be curtailed. If the site is scenically and biologically special, persuasion is easier. It also helps if the area is remote from human activity.

The Poor Knights marine reserve met all these conditions. Here, the management scheme protected existing interests, except where they were proven damaging. The site is scenically spectacular and the marine biology unique in New Zealand. The uninhabited islands lie 20 kilometres offshore, in the path of warm currents, and many tropical species live around the rocks. The fauna of the steep underwater cliffs provides colourful and exciting diving. Because the Poor Knights are so remote, there is little human activity around them apart from the divers and charter boats.

The disadvantages of this approach emerged rather slowly but became increasingly obvious. Fitting in with existing activities leaves no clear principle around which public support can rally. It is difficult to remember the necessarily complex rules and it is not easy to understand the reasons for them. Visitors expect more stringent rules, but those people who have rights of access become defensive. It is possible to step up the level of protection at a later stage, but that leads to continued argument and confusion about detailed changes to the rules. The Poor Knights marine reserve is successful as a holding action. As the area is very special and relatively undamaged, prevention of future deterioration is a worthy aim, but that is really all that has been achieved.

Ballantine, B., New Zealand's Marine Nature Reserves, *New Scientist*, 4 June 1987, p. 83.

Task 9 (Pairs)

Work in pairs, one from Group A and one from Group B. Together, decide which of the two approaches the author favours. Then check your answer by reading the conclusion below.

> At Leigh, although there was initial opposition, the more radical approach turned out to be justified. Merely by a change in management rules, an ordinary piece of coast has been transformed into an important asset to research workers, commercial fishermen, divers, tourists and the general public. The scientific, economic and social benefits of learning about the natural ecosystem and the real effects of our usual levels of exploitation are still emerging from this reserve. Plans for many more such reserves throughout the country, covering all types of marine habitats, show that New Zealand is clear about the lessons. It will be interesting to see what happens elsewhere. □

TEXT EXPLORATION

Discourse study: Identifying text structure

In the previous section, we looked at ways of identifying the main points in a text and of reducing these points to note form. Here we will look at the structure of texts and how the parts of a text relate to each other.

Texts may be divided into sections, each marked by section headings. Texts are usually further divided into paragraphs. When we come to a text, we have expectations about its structure. For example, we may expect the first paragraph to give an introduction and the last to provide a conclusion. A new paragraph may indicate a minor shift of topic and a new section a major shift.

However, these can only be expectations. A new paragraph does not always mean a new topic. A single topic may be developed over several paragraphs. A paragraph may include more than one topic. Identifying text structure helps us to understand how the topics in a text relate to each other. It also helps us to give a structure to our notes and summaries.

Task 10 (Individual, then pairs)

Study this title and the first paragraph of a text about the attempts being made to save Australia's famous koala bears from extinction.

More than one cure for extinction

A THE fight to save Australia's koalas is being waged on three fronts: in the laboratory, the forest and the political arena.

This introduction suggests that the structure of the text will fall into three main sections:

1. The role of the laboratory in the search for a cure
2. The role of the forest in the search for a cure
3. The role of the political arena in the search for a cure

Here is the rest of the text. Try to identify how the different parts of the text relate to each of these headings. Does the text follow the structure suggested in the first paragraph? Discuss your answers with your partner.

B Microbiologists are striving to identify all strains of chlamydia that affect koalas. Their goal is to develop a vaccine that can be used to protect koalas in zoos and game parks from the disease. Scientists are also attempting to find an effective treatment for infected animals.

C So far, the most promising drug is trospectomycin, an antibiotic developed in the US to treat human chlamydia. Other drugs often kill the koala along with the bacteria.

D Biologists and ecologists are collecting field data to help improve government strategies for managing the wild koalas in Australia's forests. They are evaluating the risks and benefits of moving animals from overpopulated to underpopulated areas of the country, a tactic used in the state of Victoria since the 1920s.

E Other studies are proposed to find out how much land koalas need. The amount of land needed to sustain those animals living in fragmented or sparsely wooded areas is clearly greater than in "quality" habitat, well-endowed with eucalyptus. But as yet there is no reliable method to enable ecologists to assess "quality" in this sense.

F Other biologists are investigating the koala's highly specialised digestive system to understand better the animal's nutritional requirements. This information could lead to improved diets for captive koalas. At present, they are fed eucalyptus leaves almost exclusively.

G As supplies of the leaves are not always reliable, a variety of dietary supplements would help to keep the koalas fed and fit. Experts at the University of Sydney and the Taronga Zoo in Sydney have created a "koala biscuit" that begins to fill the nutritional gap.

H Wildlife officers are encouraging land owners to safeguard koala colonies on their property, while city planners seek to "build" koalas into rapidly expanding communities. The planners are trying to introduce innovative designs that maintain good koala habitat within new residential developments; road systems that bypass koala territory or force people to drive slowly; and civic bylaws that regulate human activities and control dogs in koala country.

I Most importantly, conservationists and scientists are urging city, state and federal governments to protect koala habitat. Their message is clear: the trees cut down to make way for housing, logging and tourism, are home and kitchen to Australia's most famous marsupial. □

Deyton, L., More than one cure for extinction, Can koalas bear the twentieth century?, *New Scientist*, 26 September 1990, p. 44.

→

Task 11 (Individual, then pairs)

Using the text 'map' below try to show how the different paragraphs relate to each other.

	Paragraph(s)
Introduction	Para. A
The laboratory	
The forest	
The political arena	

Task 12 (Individual, then pairs)

Note down the key words and phrases that helped you to do Tasks 10 and 11.

Task 13 (Individual)

Complete the gaps in these notes to show the main points of the text.

Australia's approach to the problem of koala extinction

1. LAB
   Tackle prob. of disease through:
   – *identification of* (a) ....
   – *devpt of* (b) ....
   – *devpt of effective* (c) ....

2. FOREST
   Improve managemt of wild koala populatn in forest through:
   – *evaluatn of risks and benefits of movg animals from* (d) ....
   – *investign of amount of land needed to* (e) ....

3. LAB
   Improve diet of animals in captivity through:
   – *investigatn of* (f) ....
   – *devpt of* (g) ....

4. POLITICAL ARENA
   Protectn of existing koala colonies through:
   – *encouragemt of land owners to* (h) ....
   – *innovative town planning to* (i) ....
   – *bylaws to control* (j) ....
   – *pressure on city, state and federal govts to* (k) ....

Word study: Word sets

Task 14 (Individual, then pairs)

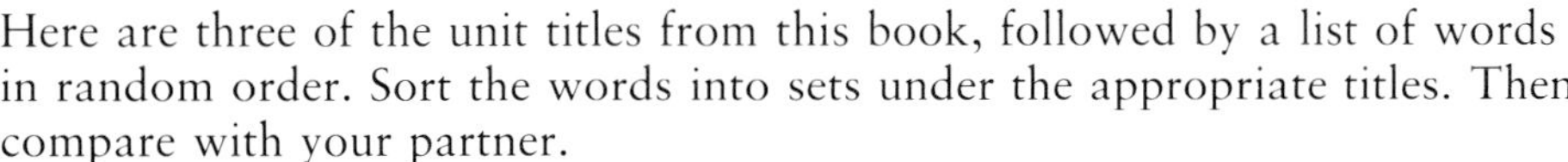

Here are three of the unit titles from this book, followed by a list of words in random order. Sort the words into sets under the appropriate titles. Then compare with your partner.

'The developing world'	'The natural world'	'The spirit of enquiry'
a) hypothesis	f) underemployment	k) literacy
b) wilderness	g) habitat	l) wildlife
c) urbanisation	h) questionnaire	m) validity
d) control group	i) migration	n) conservation
e) nature reserve	j) interview	o) preventive medicine

Now turn to the contents page and make your own word sets for the other units in this book.

APPLICATION

Task 15 (Individual)

Read this full version of the texts you studied in Task 2. Note the main points.

AT THE Institute of Zoology in London Zoo, Georgina Mace arranges marriages by computer: between Rothschild's mynahs, Arabian oryx, Siberian tigers, lowland gorillas, golden lion tamarins and scores of other rare, endangered and beautiful species. Breeding in zoos has become an essential part of conservation, but unless such breeding is carried out on a large scale, through cooperation between zoos, and between well-chosen animals, it would be bound to fail. The results would be inbred and probably infertile parodies of wild creatures that, at best, were fit only for life in captivity. The task of matchmaking is becoming so large and the orchestration so intricate that only computers can cope.

No one doubts that the ideal way to conserve animals is to do everything possible to save their habitats; the loss of wilderness, rather than the direct assault of the hunter, now endangers an estimated 25 per cent of all species. But over the past 20 years it has become clear that the mere conservation of habitat will not be enough. Even the best protected areas are usually more vulnerable than they seem, not least because they are often in areas of poverty and political instability. Hungry people at war have little time for rare animals. In the Sahel, for example, a combination of drought and human conflict has wiped out the scimitar-horned oryx.

Field studies have shown that wild animals, particularly large predators such as cheetahs and wild dogs, need far more room than anyone imagined. Population geneticists have calculated that unless animal populations are large, containing scores or hundreds of individuals, they are liable to be wiped out in the short term through drought, epidemic or  war, and are almost bound to become extinct in the longer term because of inbreeding. Some zoologists believe that only one of the populations of wild dogs of Africa is truly viable—in Botswana—and the mighty Yellowstone National Park in the US is not really big enough for its grizzly bears. It  is clear that even if the best efforts are made to save what is left of the wilderness, many animals, particularly the larger ones, will still be doomed. For many creatures captive breeding might be desirable. For many of the bigger ones in particular, it is now essential.

Breeding by numbers, Zoo datamaking – the key to success?, *New Scientist*, 1 September 1988, p. 68.

Task 16 (Individual)

Study this 'map' of the text structure. How does it compare with the main points you have noted? Use your notes to complete the gaps.

Text topic: Captive breeding for conservation

Computer matching (a) .... for conservation. *Para. 1*

Reasons:

1. small scale projects →
   (b) ....
2. conservatn nat. habitat = *Para. 2*
   (c) ....
   Reasons:
   a) vulnerable to threats,
      e.g. (d) ....
   b) areas not large enough *Para. 3*
      to (e) ....

Conclusion:

1. for many animals captive
   breeding = (f) ....
2. for bigger animals captive
   breeding = (g) ....

Task 17 (Individual)

Here is the title of the text.

Zoo datamaking – the key to success?

Explain what this title means.

The title includes a question. Is the writer's answer Yes or No? Which parts of the text help you to decide? What do you have to infer from the text to make a decision?

Unit 6 The physical world

Textbook writers use graphics for many reasons. Graphics can give a lot of information economically. One table, for instance, may save a page of words. They are also a good way of showing relationships between variables. For example, a graph could show how reading efficiency improves with time spent studying this book! Graphics are also a means of presenting both main ideas and specific details at the same time.

Graphics are used in all subjects, but are particularly common in the sciences. The texts and graphics in this unit are largely drawn from sciences and applied sciences relating to the physical world.

This unit aims to develop the reading skills required for:

1. relating texts and graphics
2. reading graphics for main ideas and specific details
3. using graphics in note-taking
4. understanding unfamiliar words

TO MAKE YOU THINK

Task 1 (Groups)

Study this diagram taken from a book called *Desertification: Its Causes and Consequences*. Discuss what the diagram shows and explain how this device works. When you have finished, read the explanatory text in the *Key* on page 154.

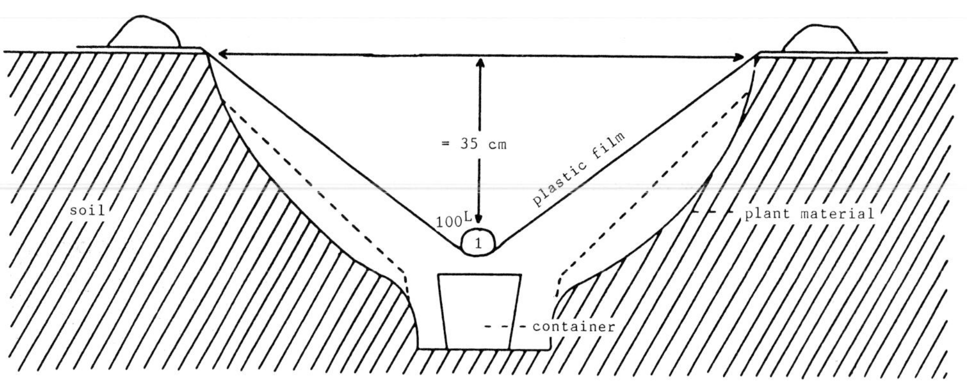

Desertification: Its Causes and Consequences (1977) UN Conference on Desertification, p. 372, Fig. 5.

Graphics sometimes stand alone, but often they have to be read with text to be understood. Both text and graphic contribute to the meaning. If we read only the graphic or only the text, we have to make much greater use of inference skills to find the meaning and we therefore increase the risk of error.

There are many different types of graphics. Here are some of the most common:

1. table
2. graph
3. flowchart
4. vertical bar chart
5. horizontal bar chart
6. piechart
7. histogram
8. schematic diagram

Task 2 (Individual, then groups)

Study these graphics from a variety of textbooks. Can you name the type of graphic? Use the list given above. Not all of these types of graphics are represented.

Try to find other examples in your textbooks.

a) **Table 2.4** Area of annual deforestation of closed broad-leaved forest in tropical regions.

	1976–80		1981–85	
	('000 ha)	(%)	('000 ha)	(%)
tropical Americas	3807	55	4006	56
tropical Africa	1319	19	1318	19
tropical Asia	1767	26	1782	25
total	6893	100	7106	100

Source: Lanly (1982, p. 82).

b)

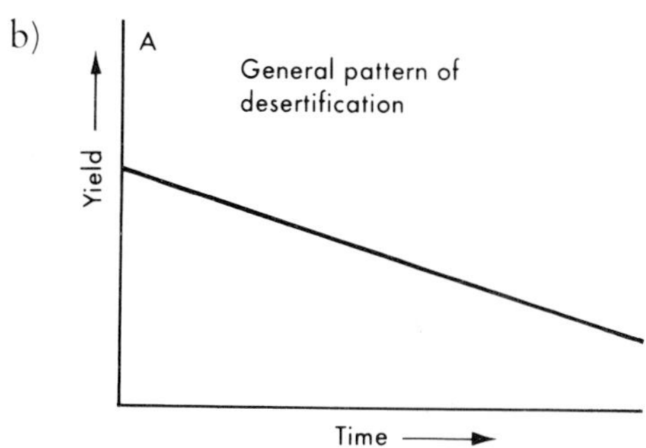

LIVERPOOL
JOHN MOORES UNIVERSITY
AVRIL ROBARTS LRC
TEL. 0151 231 4022

c)

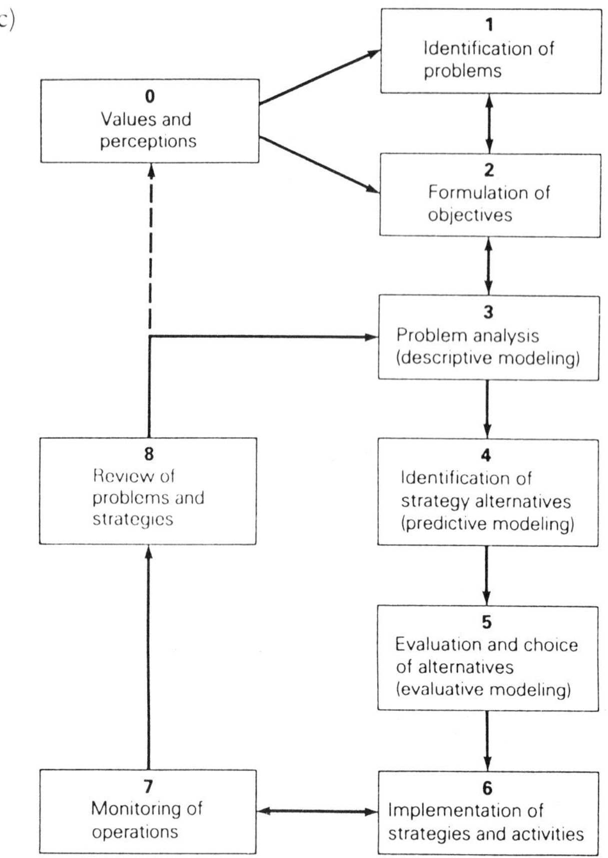

Figure 3.2 Major stages of the planning process.

d) Figure 1.4: Contributions of Various Regions to Total World Population in the Near Future

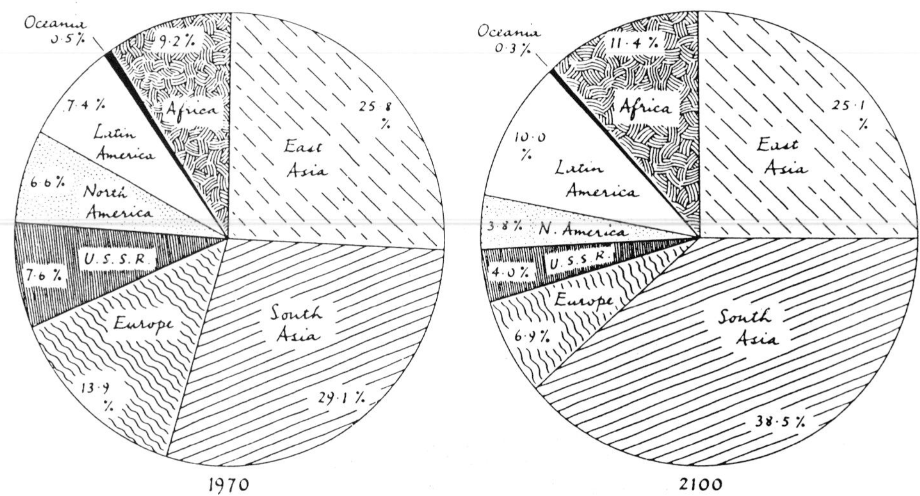

e)

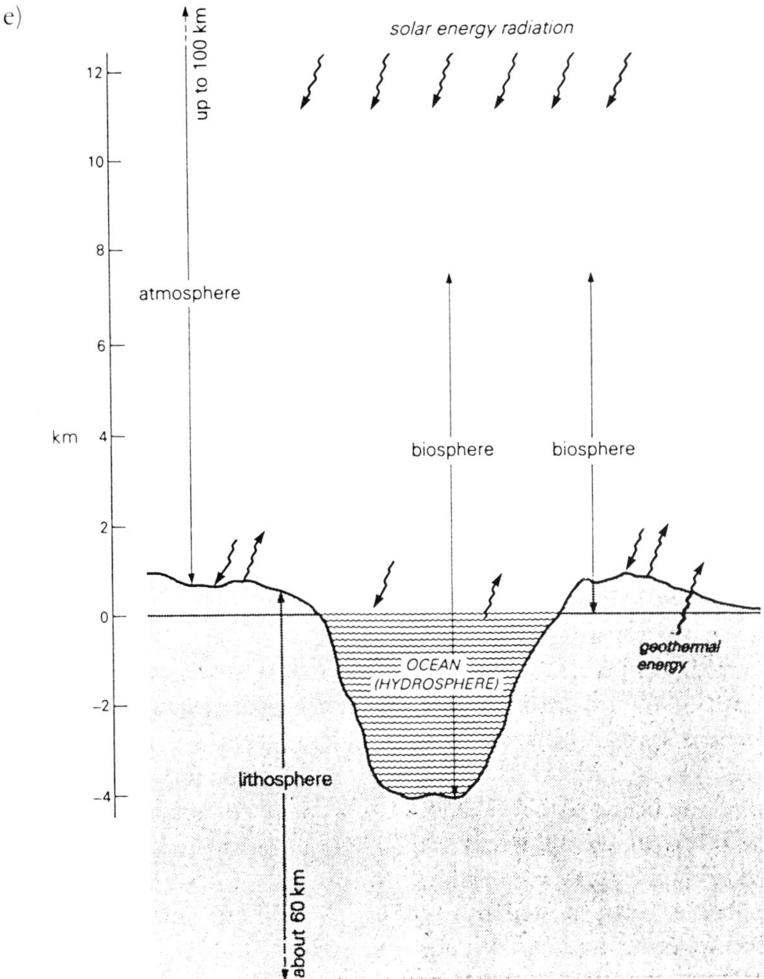

Figure 1.1 The physical world.

f)

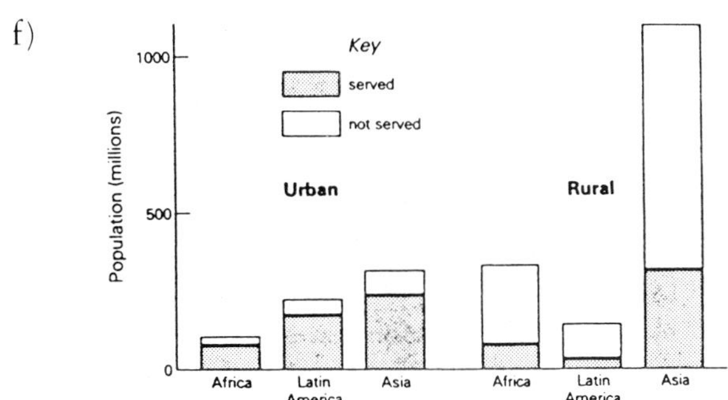

Figure 2.2 Population served with water in developing countries. (*Source*: United Nations, thirty-fifth session of the General Assembly, document A/35/367 of September 18, 1980, Table 3.)

➳

g)

MAJOR	Recycled Metric Tons	Percent of U.S. Consumption Recycled in 1979 (0% 25% 50% 75% 100%)
Lead	650,000	
Copper	550,000	
Aluminum	620,000	
Zinc	90,000	
Chromium	54,000	
Nickel	42,600	
Tin	14,200	
Antimony	31,200	
Magnesium	12,700	
MINOR		
Mercury	138	
Tungsten	1,590	
Tantalum	181	
Cobalt	900	
Selenium	95	
PRECIOUS		
Silver	1,380	
Gold	120	

a) Bartelmus, P. (1986) *Environment and Development*, p. 25 (Boston: Allen & Unwin).
b) *Desertification: Its Causes and Consequences* (1977) UN Conference on Desertification, p. 175, Fig. 2.
c) Bartelmus, P. op. cit., p. 47.
d) Waddington, C.H. (1978) *The Man-Made Future*, p. 19 (London: Croom Helm).
e) Bartelmus, P. op. cit., p. 2.
f) Bartelmus, P. op. cit., p. 24.
g) Keller, E.A. (1982) *Environmental Geology*, 3rd edition, p. 36, Fig. 12.27 (Charles E. Merrill Publishing Company).

READING AND INTERACTION

Reading graphics

We have studied how to read a text for the main idea and for specific details. Graphics too can be read in both ways. Study this histogram.

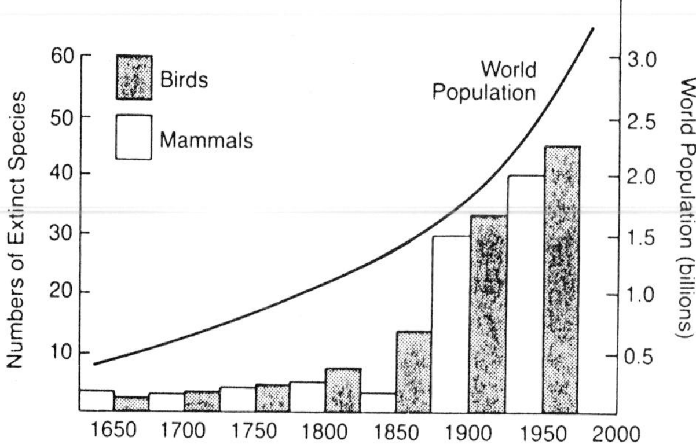

Keller, E.A. op. cit., p. 18, Fig. 2.5, *Increase in human population paralleled by increase in the extinction of birds and animals.*

Using this graphic we can find specific details for questions such as:

1. How many species of birds became extinct between 1800 and 1850?
2. What was the population of the world in 1900?
3. To what extent did world population increase between 1700 and 1800?

And at a more general level, the diagram provides the answer to this question:

4. What is the relationship between the increase in the human population and changes in the bird and animal population?

Thus, we can read this graphic for both specific details and for the main idea. Study this additional example:

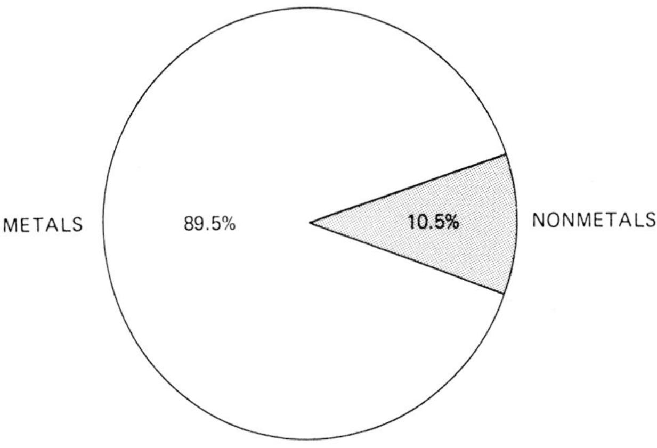

Davies, F.F. (1972) *Urban Ore*, California Geology, *Content of a typical discarded automobile.*

Main idea:	By far the largest component of a discarded automobile is metal.
Specific detail:	89.5% of a discarded automobile consists of metal.

Task 3 (Individual, then groups)

Look again at the graphics shown in Task 2. Note down a specific detail and main idea for each graphic where possible. Compare answers in your group.

Task 4 (Pairs)

Work in pairs, A and B.

Student A: Read these questions. Try to answer them with the help of the graphic below.

Student B: Read these questions. Try to answer them with the help of the text below.

How is a 'crag and tail' formation caused? Account for:

1. The origin of the rock forming the crag
2. The shape of the crag
3. The shape of the tail
4. The composition of the tail

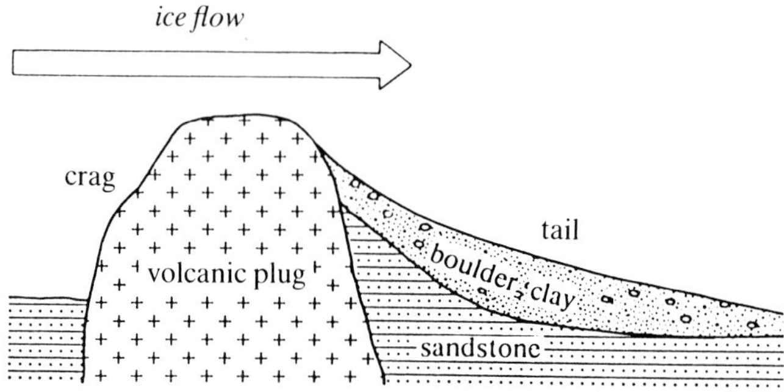

3.5.5 Deposition from ice

Erosion and deposition may occur in close proximity, not only at the margin of an area of erosion, but elsewhere on local topographic irregularities. A small hill, formed by an igneous intrusion, may be eroded by ice until a steep craggy face is left facing the ice flow; but, protected by it, a streamlined tail of softer rock or thick till is preserved on the lee side. The resultant land form (p. 180) is called a crag and tail (Fig. 3.9).

McLean, A.C. and Gribble, C.D. (1979) *Geology for Civil Engineers*, p. 73, Fig. 3.9 (London: George Allen & Unwin).

Compare your answers. Then read each other's source. Agree on the correct answers.

Task 5 (Groups)

Work in groups of three, A, B and C.

Student A: Study graphic A and answer the questions below.

Student B: Study graphic B and answer the questions below.

Student C: Study graphic C and answer the questions below.

1. What is the difference between transpiration and evaporation?
2. What is 'run-off'?
3. How does precipitation become part of ground water flow?
4. What is the most direct route for precipitation to return to the atmosphere?
5. What is magmatic water?
6. What is the water table?

Compare your answers. Now compare graphics. Which graphic provided the most complete answers?

Graphic A

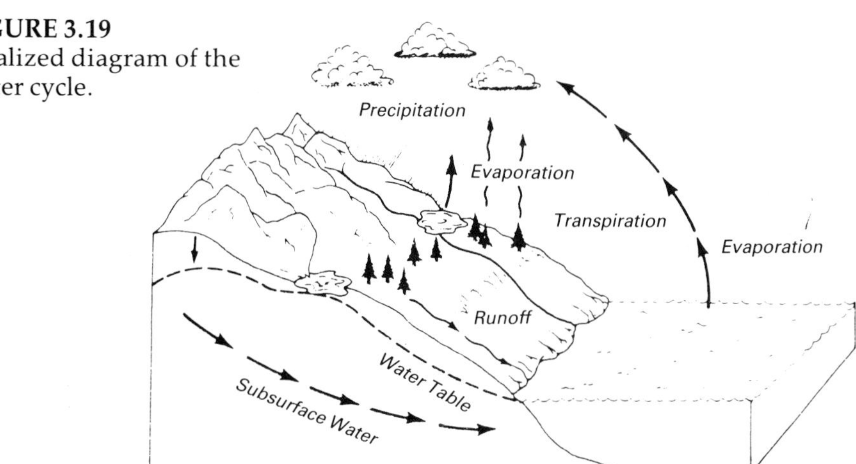

FIGURE 3.19
Idealized diagram of the water cycle.

Graphic B

Figure 2.4: The Water Cycle through the Atmosphere

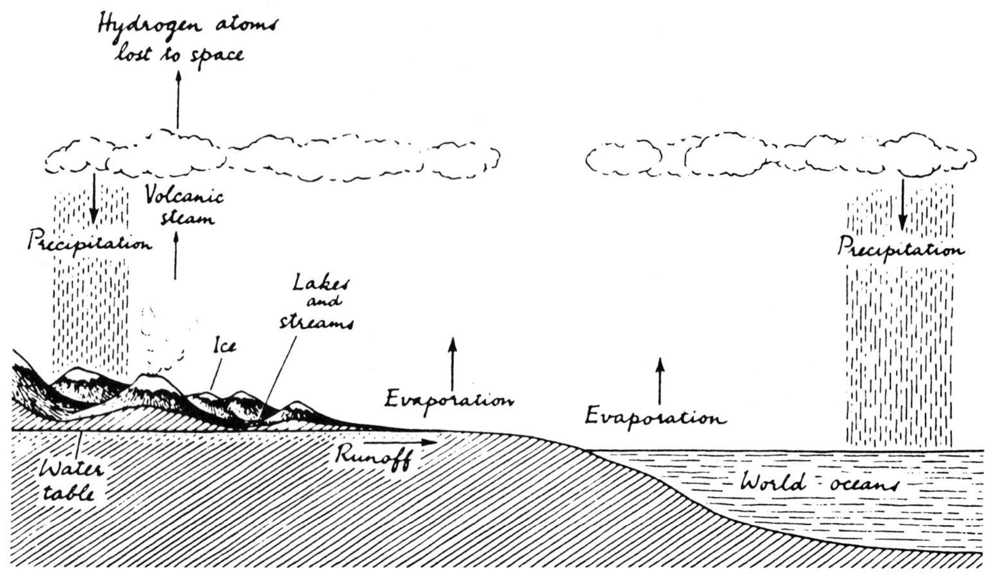

Graphic C

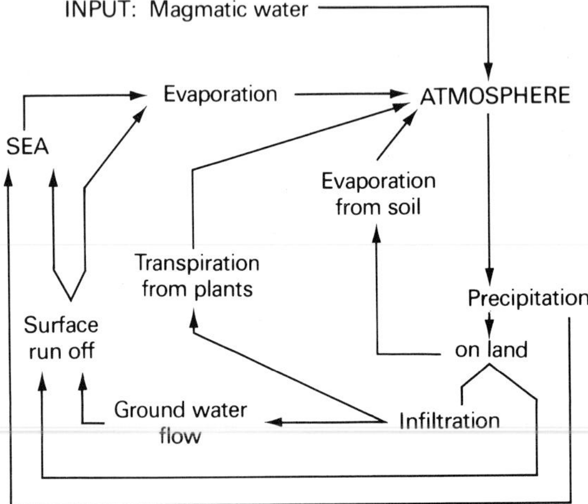

Fig. 13.1 The hydrological cycle.

A Keller, E.A. op. cit., p. 52, Fig. 3.19.
B Waddington, C.H. op. cit., p. 54, Fig. 2.4.
C Blyth, F.G.H. and de Freitas, M.H. (1984) *A Geology for Engineers*, 7th edition, p. 213, Fig. 13.1 (London: Edward Arnold).

Now check your answers using this text.

Water

The second most important constituent of the biosphere is liquid water. This can only exist in a very narrow range of temperatures, since water freezes at 0°C and boils at 100°C. This is only a tiny slice between the low temperatures of some of the other planets and the hot interior of the earth, let alone the temperature of the sun. Life as we know it would only be possible on the surface of a planet which had temperatures somewhere within this narrow range. If there is anything that can be called living on parts of the solar or other systems of the universe at a different temperature, it would have to be of an entirely different character.

The earth's supply of water probably remains fairly constant in quantity. A certain number of hydrogen atoms, which are one of the main constituents of water, are lost by escaping from the atmosphere to outer space, but they are probably just about replaced by new water brought up from the depths of the earth during volcanic action. The total quantity of water is not known very accurately, but it is about enough to cover the surface of the globe (510 million sq. km) to a depth of about two and three-quarter km. Most of it is in the form of the salt waters of the oceans – about 97 per cent. The rest is fresh, but three-quarters of this is in the form of ice at the Poles and on mountains, and cannot be used by living systems until melted. Of the remaining fraction, which is somewhat less than one per cent of the whole, there is 10–20 times as much stored as underground water as is actually on the surface. There is also a minute, but extremely important, fraction of the water supply which is present as water vapour in the atmosphere.

This tiny fraction of the water supply, existing as water vapour in the atmosphere, is the channel through which the whole water circulation of the biosphere has to pass. Water evaporated from the surface of the oceans, from lakes and rivers and from moist earth is added to it; so is the small amount from volcanoes. From it the water comes out again as rain or snow, falling on either the sea or the land. There is, as might be expected, a more intensive evaporation per unit area over the sea and oceans than over the land, but there is more precipitation over the land than over the ocean, and the balance is restored by the runoff from the land in the form of rivers.

Waddington, C.H. op. cit., pp. 52, 53.

TEXT EXPLORATION

Discourse study: Marking text structure

Simple graphics can be used to show how a text is structured. This can be useful in two ways:

1. in marking parts of the text for later revision and reference
2. in note-taking

The text on page 78 has this structure:

Text topic: Using sea water in agriculture

Introduction: problems	*Para. 1*
Methods for removing salt: problems	*Para. 2*
Evaporation methods:	
Solar methods: problems	*Para. 3*
Arizona scheme:	
Basics	*Para. 4*
Potential	*Para. 5*

We can also show this structure by using margin brackets and labels. Note how the text on page 78 has been marked. Do this only if the text belongs to you!

Discourse study: Note-taking – Spider notes

Spider notes are a useful alternative to linear notes, as they give a better visual display of the text structure. It is also simple to add supporting detail and to show links between any parts of your notes.

Study these spider notes for the text on page 78.

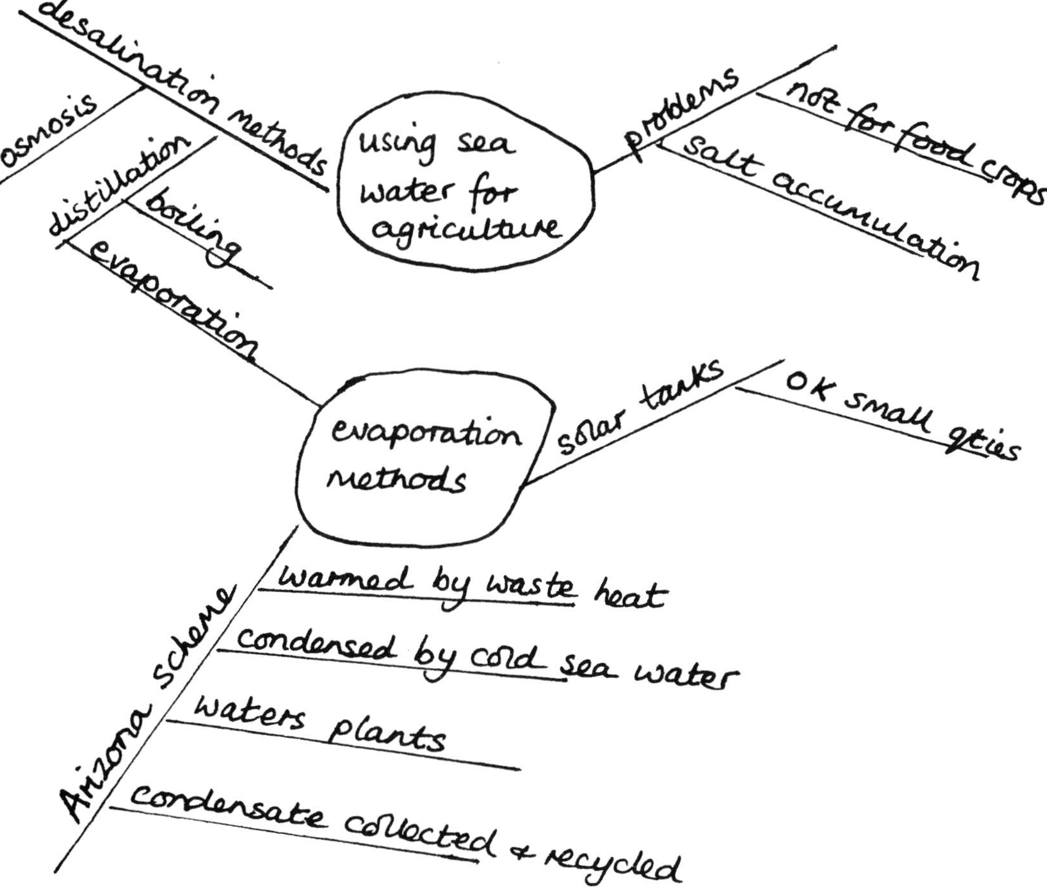

Some kinds of texts can be represented easily by rough diagrams. The kind of diagram you produce will depend on the type of text you have to deal with. For example, a text which describes a process can be represented by a flowchart. A text which classifies can be shown by a tree diagram. If quantities or percentages are given for each class, a piechart may be more suitable. A text which explains how two variables relate to each other can be represented by a graph.

Often you may have to use a mixture of graphics and more conventional notes.

Task 6 (Individual)

Show the specific details of lines 21 to 27 and lines 33 to 47 of the text on page 78 by means of rough diagrams.

LIVERPOOL
JOHN MOORES UNIVERSITY
AVRIL ROBARTS LRC
TEL. 0151 231 4022

Introduction: problems

Control of evaporation, and particularly of transpiration of water through plants, is obviously of crucial importance in all regions of the world where water is scarce. It is being investigated most thoroughly in connection with the use of sea water for agriculture. Sea water can actually be used as such for watering certain plants, on certain soils.[20] But it seems unlikely that it can be at all widely used for growing plants useful for food, and it is not at all certain how long it can be carried on before the accumulation of salt in the lower parts of the soil makes it unusable.

Methods for removing salt: problems

Most attempts to use sea water for agriculture depend on first removing the excess salt. There are two basic methods of desalination. One depends on using a membrane which will allow the water to pass, but will hold back the salts (reversed osmosis). The other is distillation, that is to say water vapour or steam is produced and this, which does not contain salts, forms fresh water when it is condensed. The production of steam can be done by actually boiling the sea water or, more gently, by encouraging evaporation from the surface of sea water which is warmed but not raised to boiling point. Both the membrane-filtering techniques and the boiling technique require large amounts of concentrated energy. They are essentially industrial processes of a very energy-consuming kind. The evaporation methods are much less demanding, and I will discuss them first.

Evaporation methods

Solar methods: problems

The cheapest way of evaporating sea water is to use the heat of the sun. The sea water is run into shallow tanks of concrete or plastic, preferably with a black bottom which absorbs the sun's heat. The tanks, which are usually built long and narrow, are covered with a transparent roof with curved or sloping sides. The water in the tanks is warmed, evaporates, and the water vapour condenses again on the cooler glass roof and runs down the sides to be collected in a trough at the bottom. Installations of this kind are already in use in many arid regions near the sea, from the coasts of Chile to the Aegean islands. It is a very satisfactory process provided one does not want too much water. It has mostly been used to provide drinking water. The quantities required for agricultural irrigation would require enormous areas of tanks.

Arizona scheme

Basics

A much more sophisticated low temperature evaporation scheme is being developed in Arizona.[21] The scheme involves using cold sea water which is pumped into the installation to aid the condensation of the water vapour which has been produced by hot sea water. Originally solar energy was used to heat the sea water, but since any place that wanted to run such a scheme would certainly be generating its own electricity, probably with a diesel engine, use was later made of the 'waste heat' in the cooling water of the engine.

Potential

They also introduced another improvement which is of very general application. The fresh water was used on plants grown in plastic greenhouses. A large sheet of plastic is attached to a low brick or stone wall, and a small pump keeps the air pressure inside the plastic at about half a pound per square foot, above the air pressure outside, so the plastic is inflated, in the form of a long low sausage. The plastic is transparent to the sunlight which the plants need, while the water, led to the plant roots and transpired through their leaves, is trapped inside and not allowed to escape back into the general atmosphere; it can be used again and again. Experimental plants of this kind are working in Arizona and Mexico, and a quite big one, planned to provide food for a sizeable population, is being built in the oil-rich Persian Gulf state of Abu Dhabi. There are quite a large number of areas in the world in which arid deserts come near enough to the sea coast for developments of this kind to make important contributions to the world's food supply.

Waddington, C.H. op. cit., pp. 98–100.

Word study: Using the wider context

In Units 2 and 3 we studied how to work out the meaning of a word by identifying the kind of word and using its immediate context, the sentence in which the word occurs. Try to work out the meaning of the words in **bold** type using these methods.

1. Many phenomena produce sound in an **incidental** but unavoidable fashion.
2. These usually have two primary components: a mechanism for producing a vibration and a **resonant structure**.

In these cases, the immediate context may not give you enough help. It is necessary then to look at the wider context for more clues. Underline the parts of this text which help you with the meaning of 'incidental'.

Sound Sources

Many phenomena produce sound in an incidental but unavoidable fashion. For example, the combustion of fuel in an engine always produces some sound as a by-product. This sound is both annoying and wasteful of energy. However, there are many man-made and natural sources for which sound is the desired output. These usually have two primary components: a mechanism for producing a vibration and a resonant structure.

The second sentence tells us that sound made by burning fuel in an engine is an example of sound produced in an incidental fashion – as a by-product. By joining this information from the wider context of the text with our own knowledge – that fuel is burned in an engine to produce power, not sound – we find that 'incidental' means here 'unplanned'.

For 'resonant structure' we have to look at a wider context – the next paragraph of the text. Which parts of this paragraph help you know the meaning of this term?

Musical instruments present a variety of arrangements for the production of sound. In a violin the strings vibrate, and their vibrations are efficiently transmitted to the air by the resonant hollow body of the instrument. In woodwinds and brasses the vibrations are produced by causing the air in the mouthpiece to puff, swirl, and eddy. This causes the reeds in woodwinds to vibrate. In brasses the lips themselves vibrate as air is blown in the mouthpiece. In both cases the oscillatory flow of air results in standing waves in the extended hollow body of the instrument, and the energy is then efficiently transmitted to the air outside. Similarly the oral and nasal cavities in humans serve as resonant structures for vibrations produced by the vocal cords.

Kane, J.W. and Sternheim, M.M. (1984) *Physics*, 2nd edition, p. 452 (Chichester: John Wiley & Sons).

Task 7 (Individual, then groups)

Find approximate meanings for these words as used in the text on page 79. Use any of the methods we have covered.

1. brasses (lines 11, 13)
2. eddy (line 12)
3. cavities (line 17)

Compare meanings with your group. Discuss how you decided on these meanings.

Task 8 (Individual)

Graphics are part of the wider context you can use when searching for the meaning of unfamiliar words. Underline the terms in this text which are explained by the graphics which accompany it.

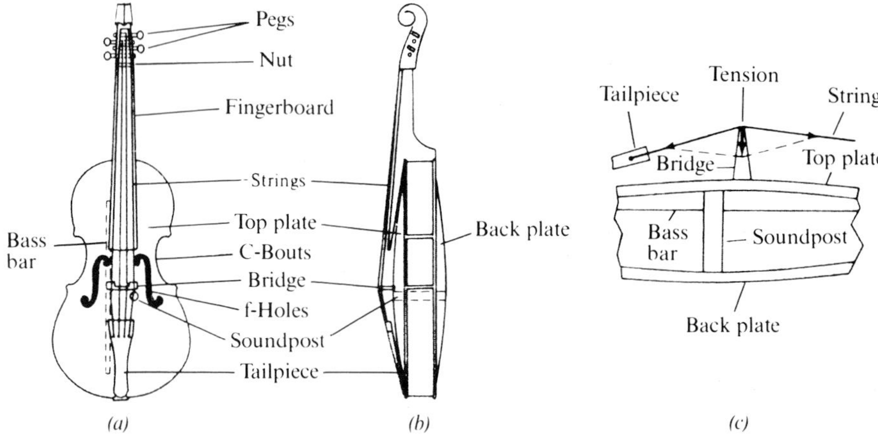

Figure 22.8 *(a)* Front and *(b)* side views of a violin. *(c)* An enlarged view of the bridge and part of the violin body.

The Violin | The body of a violin is a more complex resonant structure than the tube. When the strings of a violin are plucked or bowed, their vibrations are transferred to the body through the bridge (Fig. 22.8). Although the strings may vibrate with many different frequency components, the body resonates at and amplifies only certain frequencies.

The violin body vibrates so that its volume varies, and air is forced in and out through the f-holes. This is called the air resonance. The front and back plates of the body can also vibrate at characteristic frequencies called body resonances. Just as a string can vibrate at more than one frequency, so also can the violin plates, and several body resonances exist (Fig. 22.9). The frequencies of the air and body resonances should be at or near the fundamental string frequencies. If this is not achieved some notes will be muted or distorted.

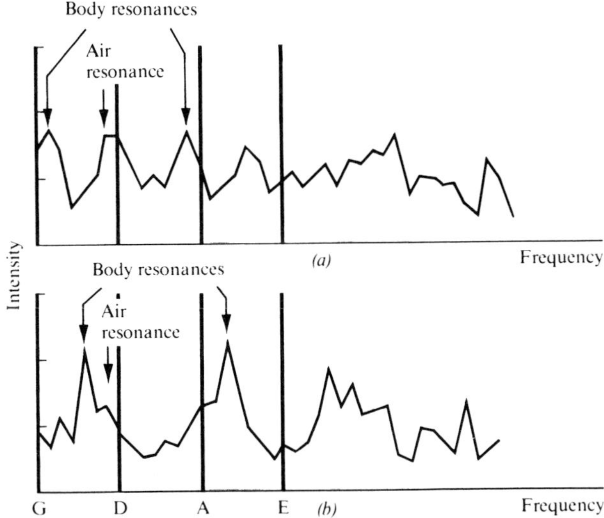

Figure 22.9 *(a)* The intensity-versus-frequency graph for a good violin. The vertical lines represent the characteristic frequencies of the four violin strings. Note that the resonances occur at nearly the same frequencies as those characteristic of the strings. *(b)* The spectrum of a poor violin.

Kane, J.W. and Sternheim, M.M. op. cit., pp. 453–4.

Grammar and meaning: Hypothetical WOULD

You are probably familiar with *would* in *if*-sentences like this:

If the ice caps melted, the sea would flood many parts of the world.

The combination of *If* and *would* clearly shows that the statement is hypothetical. It describes potential, not real events. However, *would* is often used by itself and it can be more difficult to separate real from hypothetical statements. Compare:

1. We require very large solar cells to power ships. =*Such cells exist. We can do it.*
2. We would require very large solar cells to power ships. =*Such cells do not exist. We cannot do it.*

Compare:

3. Using distilled sea water for irrigation requires enormous evaporation tanks. =*This is fact and current practice.*
4. Using distilled sea water for irrigation would require enormous evaporation tanks. =*This is theoretically possible, but not practical.*

Task 9 (Individual, then pairs)

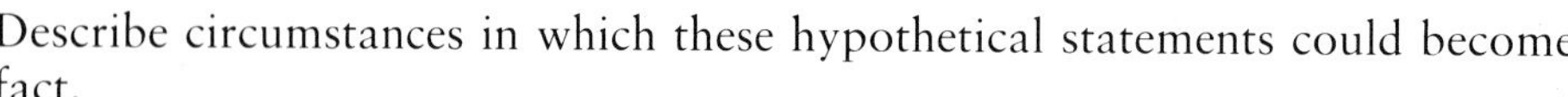

Describe circumstances in which these hypothetical statements could become fact.

1. Icebergs would provide a source of fresh water for countries in the Middle East with water problems.
2. Life as we know it would be possible on other planets.
3. Reclaiming desert areas would enable this planet to support an even larger population.
4. Massive sea walls would protect low-lying countries from tidal waves.
5. Recycling 50% of glass products would lead to energy saving.

APPLICATION

Task 10 (Individual)

Complete this table using the specific details in this text.

Liquid	*Volume (km^3)*	*% of world total*
TOTAL		

Describe the main idea represented by this table in one sentence.

5. Wide places in rivers

Lakes have been called wide places in rivers. This is true of many small lakes that are impounded by relatively minor and geologically temporary obstructions across river channels. But no single over-simplified metaphor accurately describes all lakes, which vary widely in their physical characteristics and in the geological circumstances under which they occur. The handsome little tarn occupying an ice-scooped basin in the glaciated Alps differs radically from the deep and limpid Crater Lake of Oregon, occupying the collapsed crater of an extinct volcano. The North American Great Lakes occupy huge basins formed in a complex manner by isostatic subsidence of that whole region of the earth's crust, glacial excavation, moraine and outwash deposition, and other factors. These lakes have no resemblance to Lake Tanganyika in the great Rift Valley of Africa, where geological processes created the rift by literally pulling two sections of the earth's crust apart, opening a deep gash, part of which is occupied by the lake. The world contains many other spectacular examples of genetically different lakes.

The earth's land areas are dotted with hundreds of thousands of lakes. Areas like Wisconsin–Minnesota and Finland each contain some tens of thousands. But these small lakes, important though they may be locally, contain only a minor amount of the world supply of fresh surface water, most of which is in a relatively few large lakes on three continents.

The aggregate volume of all fresh-water lakes in the world is about 125,000 km^3, and their surface area is about 825,000 km^2. About 80% of the water is in forty large lakes. For the purpose of this chapter a lake is called large if its contents are 10 km^3 or more. Thus the group excludes water bodies such as the Zürichsee of Switzerland (about 4 km^3). The range of volume among the 'large' lakes is enormous, from the lower limit of about 10 km^3 in Lake Okeechobee (Florida) to an upper limit of nearly 22,000 km^3 in Lake Baikal (central Asia), the world's bulkiest and deepest single body of fresh water. The latter contains nearly as much water as the five Great Lakes of North America. The latter are large in surface area, but their average depth is very much less than that of Baikal.

The Great Lakes and other large lakes in North America contain about 32,000 km^3 of water, which is a fourth of all the liquid fresh surface water in existence. Large lakes of Africa contain 36,000 km^3, or nearly 30% of the earth's total. Asia's Lake Baikal alone contains about 18% of the total.

Lakes on these three continents account for more than 70% of the world's fresh surface water. Large lakes on other continents – Europe, South America, and Australia – contain a comparatively small amount, about 3,000 km^3, or roughly 2% of the total. About a fourth of the total fresh surface-water supply occurs in the hundreds of thousands of rivers and lesser lakes throughout the world.

Chorley, R.J. (1969) *Water, Earth and Man*, p. 36 (London: Methuen).

Unit 7 Into the future

A constant need in any discipline is to keep up with developments in your field, to be up-to-date. The texts in this unit look into the future and examine likely developments in areas which concern us all.

When we study, we draw our ideas from a variety of sources. As we saw in Unit 6, our sources may include graphics as well as texts.

This unit aims to develop the reading skills we need to:

1. locate information in different sources
2. compare information from different sources

TO MAKE YOU THINK

Task 1 (Groups)

Predict developments in these areas in the next 25 years.

1. Jobs
2. Growth of cities
3. Global warming
4. Food production

Task 2 (Groups)

Study these texts from a journal. What predictions do they make? How do these compare with your own predictions?

a)

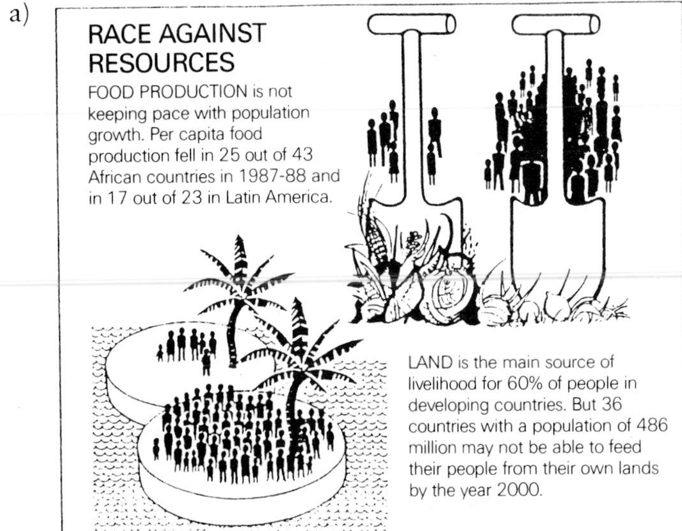
RACE AGAINST RESOURCES
FOOD PRODUCTION is not keeping pace with population growth. Per capita food production fell in 25 out of 43 African countries in 1987-88 and in 17 out of 23 in Latin America.
LAND is the main source of livelihood for 60% of people in developing countries. But 36 countries with a population of 486 million may not be able to feed their people from their own lands by the year 2000.

b)

WARMING

- By the middle of the next century average world temperatures will rise by 1.5-2.8 degrees C. The world will be hotter than at any time during the previous 120,000 years.
- Melting ice and thermal evaporation may cause the sea level to rise by up to 70cms by the middle of the 21st century, causing serious flooding in low-lying areas. A 50-centimetre sea-level rise would displace 16% of Egypt's population. Most of the Republic of the Maldives would disappear – the islands' highest point is less than 2 metres above sea level.

c)

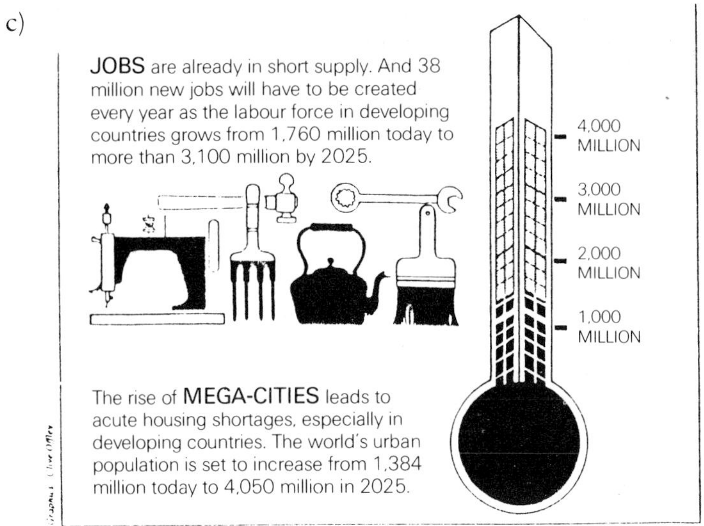

JOBS are already in short supply. And 38 million new jobs will have to be created every year as the labour force in developing countries grows from 1,760 million today to more than 3,100 million by 2025.
4,000 MILLION
3,000 MILLION
2,000 MILLION
1,000 MILLION
The rise of MEGA-CITIES leads to acute housing shortages, especially in developing countries. The world's urban population is set to increase from 1,384 million today to 4,050 million in 2025.

Population growth, can it be slowed down? *Developing World*, The Courier, No. 123, Sept.–Oct. 1990, pp. 89–90.

Task 3 (Individual, then groups)

What are your feelings about the future? Write down a list of words and phrases that you associate with the word 'FUTURE'. Put them under two headings – *Positive* and *Negative*.

Compare them with the rest of your group; then the rest of your class. On balance, are the feelings of your class mainly positive or mainly negative?

READING AND INTERACTION

Comparing sources

When we consult several sources we should have a clear purpose. This may include:

1. clarifying something we are not sure about
2. checking the accuracy of our information
3. getting additional information on a topic
4. comparing viewpoints on a topic

It helps to have specific questions in mind before comparing sources. These help to guide us to the information we need. In this section we will compare sources that provide us with factual information.

Task 4 (Individual, then class)

When we think about the future, we usually think about the role of science and technology. Conduct a survey to find the views of your class on the importance of science and technology to the future of your country and the world. Use the questionnaire on the next page:

1. Do you believe that many of the world's problems can be solved by scientific research?
2. Do you believe that science and technology play a major role in our lives?
3. Do you believe that your country's national prosperity depends on science and technology?
4. Do you think that it is important for your country to be a leading nation in science?
5. Do you believe that politicians know enough to judge the importance of science and technology?

Answer using this scale:

	Questions 1	2	3	4	5
Agree strongly					
Agree					
Neither agree nor disagree					
Disagree					
Strongly disagree					
Don't know					

Task 5 (Individual)

Compare these tables which report some of the findings of two surveys conducted in the United Kingdom. Your purpose is to:

1. Compare the questions asked
2. Compare the results
3. Make conclusions from this comparison

Table 1

'Overall do science and technology do more good than harm, more harm than good, or about the same of each?'

	Totals %
More good than harm	44
More harm than good	9
About equal	37
Don't know	10

Gallup Poll conducted on behalf of *New Scientist* June/July 1989 and reported in *New Scientist*, 16th September 1989.

Table 2

'The benefits of science are greater than any harmful effects.'

	Totals %
Agree strongly	11.8
Agree	33
Neither agree nor disagree	17.4
Disagree	21.6
Disagree strongly	10.2
Don't know	6

Oxford University Department for External Studies, published in *Nature*, Vol. 340, p. 11.

Task 6 (Individual)

Now read this text which compares the two studies. Does it identify the same similarities and differences that you have noted?

The Oxford study also provides a number of checks with our own survey. For example, in a long list of questions, the survey team asked people to respond to the statement: "The benefits of science are greater than any harmful effects." While the question isn't quite the same as that we asked (Table 1), and the results are presented differently, the sentiment is similar. On a scale of 5 (agree strongly) to 1 (disagree strongly), 44·8 per cent agreed (11·8 per cent strongly), 17·4 per cent were in the middle and 31·8 per cent disagreed (10·2 per cent strongly)—the rest (6·0 per cent) "don't know". In our survey, 44 per cent thought that science does more good than harm, while a larger number (37 per cent) were in the middle (about equal).

Science stays up the poll, *New Scientist*, 16 September 1989, p. 57.

Task 7 (Class)

Compare your own poll with the results from the two studies.

TEXT EXPLORATION

Discourse study: Comparing text structures

In this section we are going to compare two texts on the 'Human genome programme' to see how similar they are in terms of structure and the information they present. The 'Human genome programme' has been described as biology's first big science project.

Task 8 (Individual, then pairs)

Here is the first text in jumbled order. Try to put the paragraphs in the correct order. Note the words and phrases that help you.

Text 1

A But making sense of this information will be a complicated task, partly because of the sheer quantity of data the project will churn out. The genome comprises 3500 million molecular groups known as "bases", or nucleotides. These are known as A (adenine), C (cytosine), T (thymine) and G (guanine). When arranged in sequences of tens of thousands of bases, maybe more, these nucleotides represent genes. These genes are arranged on chromosomes, of which each individual has 46 arranged in pairs. There are 24 different chromosomes, including the two sex chromosomes.

B Such a present might well be feasible by then, although for most people it would have value only as a novelty item. Even for the scientist, the genome of one individual would not be ideal. What medical science needs is a generalised genome, the genetic equivalent of the generalised skeleton used to depict our anatomy, based on DNA instead of bone.

C It is the year 2050, and you are flicking through a booklet of advertisements for the latest gadgets, looking for a present for the friend who has everything. You spot it; a compact disc holding their complete genome – a personal record of the DNA that helps to mould their physical and mental characteristics.

D The human genome project is a £2 billion venture involving scientists from around the globe. Stretching over the next 15 years at least, the project aims to produce just such a generalised genome, from which geneticists will try to establish the differences between individuals and "the norm". Biochemists will use the sequence to plan novel genetically engineered organisms that can produce scarce, medically useful human proteins and hormones. Doctors and researchers will use the clues in our DNA to discover, diagnose, understand and treat human genetic diseases.

Watts, S., Making sense of the genome's secrets, *New Scientist*, 4 August 1990, p. 37.

Now compare your ideas with this text 'map'.

Text topic: The human genome project

Introduction: Definition of genome	*Para. 1*
'generalised genome'	*Para. 2*
Description of 'Human genome project': Cost Timescale Aims	*Para. 3*
Applications by: a) geneticists b) biochemists c) doctors and researchers	
Problem: Quantity of information	*Para. 4*

Task 9 (Individual)

Read through the text again. Using the text 'map' as an outline, make notes of the important points.

Task 10 (Individual, then pairs)

Here is the second text in jumbled order. Try to put the paragraphs in the correct order. Note the words and phrases that help you.

Text 2

A The speed with which tentative suggestion was transformed into a multi-million-dollar-a-year programme, indicates that it was an idea whose time had come. Technically, it was on the cusp of feasibility. More important still, it captured the imagination of those American legislators who are extremely keen to boost their country's competitiveness in the burgeoning field of biotechnology.

B Compared with the huge amounts of money that governments have traditionally poured into physical science projects – $30 billion for the Space Station and nearly $8 billion for the Superconducting Supercollider, for instance – the $3 billion price tag for knowing everything there is to know about the genetic make up of *Homo sapiens* seems modest. Still, this is heady stuff for biologists, many of whom are exhilarated by the prospect, while many others are fearful of what it might do to traditional or "small science" biology.

C In a mere five years, mapping and sequencing the human genome – the DNA in all 24 chromosomes – has gone from the stuff of dreams to a massively funded program in the US. If this effort proceeds as expected, within the next five years it will be possible to pinpoint any region on this vast genetic landscape: this is the map. And within a further 10 years it will be possible to read from beginning to end virtually every one of the 3 billion genetic letters that make up the genome: this is the sequence. It will cost about $3 billion and tens of thousands of man hours. The Human Genome Program is, unquestionably, biology's first "big science" project.

Lewin, R., In the beginning was the genome, *New Scientist*, 21 July 1990, p. 34.

Now compare your ideas with this text 'map'.

Text topic: The human genome program

Aims Definition Timescale Cost	*Para. 1*
cf. Physical science projects Biologists' attitudes to program	*Para. 2*
Reasons for adoption of program	*Para. 3*

Task 11 (Individual, then pairs)

Compare the text maps. What differences and similarities are there in the structure of the two texts?

Read through the text again. Using the text 'map' as an outline, make notes of the important points. Then compare your notes on the two texts. What differences and similarities are there in the information you have noted?

Grammar and meaning: Degrees of certainty

In this unit we have read about predictions. The language used tells us how certain the writer is about these predictions.

This table indicates degrees of certainty on a scale of 1–6.

1. Certain (positive)	*is, will, must*
2. Strong possibility (positive)	*may/might/could well*
3. Possibility (positive)	*may, might, could*
4. Possibility (negative)	*may not, might not*
5. Strong possibility (negative)	*may/might well not*
6. Certain (negative)	*is/will not, cannot*

Task 12 (Individual, then pairs)

Use the scale to indicate the writer's degree of certainty for each of these statements from texts in this unit.

1. Such a present might well be feasible by then.
2. The human genome program is a $2 billion program.
3. Doctors will use clues in our DNA to discover, diagnose and treat human genetic disease.
4. Food production is not keeping pace with population growth.
5. Melting ice and thermal expansion may cause the sea to rise by the middle of the 21st century.
6. Thirty-six countries with a population of 486 million may not be able to feed their people from their own lands by the year 2000.
7. The world's population is set to increase to 4050 million in 2025.

Word study: Word structure

The last step in working out the meaning of an unfamiliar word is to look for clues in the structure of the word. Study this example:

uncertainty

We can break it down into its components like this:

		Word class	*Meaning*
Root	certain	adjective	sure
+suffix	certain + ty	noun	sureness
+prefix	un + certainty	noun	not being sure

Working out the meaning of a word from its structure can only be done with a minority of English words. Use this method once you have tried all the other ways of identifying an unfamiliar word. Be careful. Some apparent prefixes are in fact part of the root. Compare, for example, 'restart' and 'respect'.

One way to remember English affixes (prefixes and suffixes) is to make your own checklist. For example:

Affix	*Meaning*	*Added to*	*Examples*
en – – en	make/cause	adjectives	ensure soften

Try these examples from texts you have read in this book:

inactive	transformed
disproportionate	employment
reintroduced	futility
improbable	desalination
irrelevance	shortening
unquestionably	standardise

We can summarise our approach to unfamiliar words as follows:

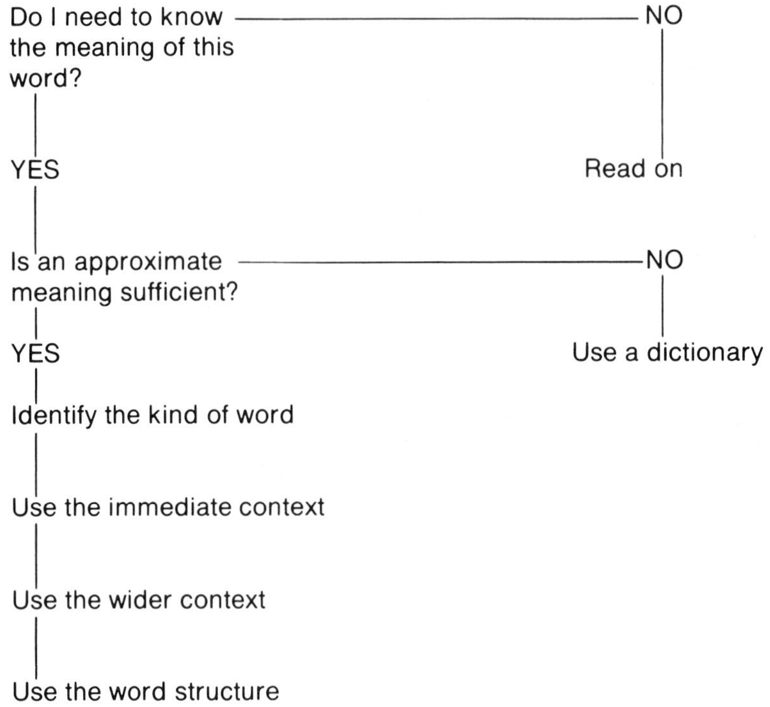

Do I need to know the meaning of this word?
NO
Read on
YES
Is an approximate meaning sufficient?
NO
Use a dictionary
YES
Identify the kind of word
Use the immediate context
Use the wider context
Use the word structure

APPLICATION

Task 13 (Individual)

Study this list of points from a text about the 'Human genome project'. The points are not in order. Now read the text and arrange the points in the correct order.

1. Strengths of UK approach
2. Reasons for UK involvement
3. UK funding
4. Recommended strategy
5. Definition of human genome
6. US commitment
7. Expected cost of US research

Britain and the human genome

As Americans with megabucks gear up to unravel the secrets of human genetics, can British scientists do anything useful with a relatively modest sum?

John Galloway

THE human genome is about a metre of DNA containing three billion pairs of chemical building blocks known as bases. The American government has committed itself to discovering the sequence of bases in this DNA. Sequencing DNA now costs between $3 (£1.75) and $5 per base pair, so the project will probably cost more than $10 billion.

And what about Britain's contribution to the project? With classic British understatement, the government has agreed to support a British project to map the human genome by supplementing the Medical Research Council's grant-in-aid by £11 million over three years.

Can anything be done with £11 million in the face of this colossal American effort and the possibility of a corresponding effort by the Japanese? Is it worth doing anything at all?

Involvement with the genome project is important for Britain. Whoever gets the human genome data first will decide what will happen to them, and will be in an unassailable position to dictate terms over its commercial, including its medical, exploitation. Britain has to buy itself a seat at the international bargaining table, and we will probably have less than five years to establish our credentials. Bidding will not wait for the project to be completed – it will start as soon as there is anything worth selling.

Given the competitiveness of the human genome game, is the £11 million enough to ensure that Britain is taken seriously? In all probability, yes, provided that the money is spent imaginatively. A subtle, finely tuned approach may still mean that British research is world-class, even if it is relatively poorly funded.

The strength of the British approach lies in its potential to put the powerful techniques of molecular genetics into the hands of people who have an important biological problem to solve. So the best strategy, at least for Britain's small-scale studies, is to find a way of ensuring that research groups with interesting biological, commercial or medical problems have help with the methodology and technology of molecular genetics. Rather than having a methodology looking for applications, we should ensure that anyone with a good problem has access to this methodology.

Galloway, J., Britain and the human genome, *New Scientist*, 28 July, 1990, p. 41.

LIVERPOOL
JOHN MOORES UNIVERSITY
AVRIL ROBARTS LRC
TEL. 0151 231 4022

Task 14 (Individual)

Make a text 'map' similar to those you have studied in this unit. Use the ordered list of points to help you.

Unit 8 The individual and society

This unit and Unit 9 aim to develop the skills of critical reading. 'Critical reading' means testing the strength of an argument, proposal or explanation in a text. It also means measuring the ideas in a text against your own ideas and against those of other writers. Critical reading is an important skill for any student, but is of particular importance to the social scientist because sociology is a subject in which conflicting viewpoints are common. For this reason, social science has been described as an 'argumentative subject'. The texts in this unit are drawn from social science sources.

TO MAKE YOU THINK

Task 1 (Individual, then groups)

Study these statements about education. Divide them into facts and opinions. Compare your answers with your group. Discuss how you can recognise a fact and how an opinion.

1. In the United States the per capita costs of schooling have risen almost as fast as the cost of medical treatment.
2. Equal obligatory schooling must be recognised as at least economically unfeasible.
3. Paradoxically, the belief that universal schooling is absolutely necessary is most firmly held in those countries where the fewest people have been – and will be – served by schools.
4. We have all learned most of what we know outside school.
5. A good educational system should provide all who want to learn with access to available resources at any time in their lives.
6. I believe that a desirable future depends on our deliberately choosing a life of action over a life of consumption.
7. The university graduate has been schooled for selective service among the rich of the world.
8. Half the people in our world never set foot in school.
9. School groups people according to age.
10. Schools create jobs for schoolmasters, no matter what their pupils learn from them.

Illich, I.D. (1971) *Deschooling Society* (London: Calder and Boyars).

Task 2 (Individual, then pairs)

Work in pairs.

Student A: Note down points to use in an argument to support this statement.
Student B: Note down points to use in an argument to oppose this statement.

> Even with schools of equal quality, a poor child can seldom catch up with a rich one.

Student As now work with another Student A, and Student Bs work with another Student B. You have each prepared the same argument. Read each other's points. Try to agree on the best argument.

Now form pairs with Students A and B working together. You have each prepared opposing arguments. Try to find faults in each other's argument.

Task 3 (Groups)

Discuss in your group what makes a persuasive argument.

Task 4 (Individual)

Now study this argument. Does it persuade you to agree with the writer?

> It should be obvious that even with schools of equal quality a poor child can seldom catch up with a rich one. Even if they attend equal schools and begin at the same age, poor children lack most of the educational opportunities which are casually available to the middle-class child. These advantages range from conversation and books in the home to vacation travel and a different sense of oneself, and apply, for the child who enjoys them, both in and out of school. So the poorer student will generally fall behind so long as he depends on school for advancement or learning.
>
> Illich, I.D. op. cit., p. 6.

READING AND INTERACTION

Critical reading

A first step in critical reading is to break down the argument into points. You can do this in your head or by making notes like these on the text in Task 4:

1. Even with equal schools, poor child cannot catch up with rich
2. ∵ Lack m/c educational opportunities
3. e.g. conversation & books at home
   vacation travel
   diff. sense self
4. Apply in/out school
5. ∴ Poor child falls behind if depends school

Then ask yourself these questions:

1. Are all the points supported (or are some just assertions)?
2. Are unsupported points either known facts or generally accepted opinions?
3. If a point is supported by examples, are they well-chosen?
4. Does the conclusion follow logically from the points?

Task 5 (Individual)

Half the class should read Text 1 and the other half read Text 2. The notes which follow your text summarise the points of the argument. Show how the points are linked by completing the blanks in the notes with the appropriate symbol or word from this list:

∵ because	ALTHO' although
∴ therefore	BUT
& and	ALSO in addition
e.g. for example	

Text 1

A second major illusion on which the school system rests is that most learning is the result of teaching. Teaching, it is true, may contribute to certain kinds of learning under certain conditions. But most people acquire most of their knowledge outside school, and in school only insofar as school, in a few rich countries, has become their place of confinement during an increasing part of their lives.

Most learning happens casually, and even most intentional learning is not the result of programmed instruction. Normal children learn their first language casually, although faster if their parents pay attention to them. Most people who learn a second language well do so as a result of odd circumstances and not of sequential teaching. They go to live with their grandparents, they travel, or they fall in love with a foreigner. Fluency in reading is also more often than not a result of such extracurricular activities. Most people who read widely, and with pleasure, merely believe that they learned to do so in school; when challenged, they easily discard this illusion.

Illich, I.D. op cit., p. 12.

1. Most learning NOT because teaching.
2. .... Teaching may help in s. conditions.
3. .... Most knowledge out/s school.
4. .... In/s school only insofar as confined there.
5. Most learning casual (not intentional).
6. .... 1st lang. learnt casually.
7. Even most intentional learning NOT because teaching.

8. .... If 2nd lang. learnt well, learnt because odd circumstances like travel.
9. .... Fluent reading because out/s school activities.
10. Good readers merely believe learned at school.
11. .... When challenged, discard this illusion.

Text 2

Equal obligatory schooling must be recognised as at least economically unfeasible. In Latin America the amount of public money spent on each graduate student is between 350 and 1,500 times the amount spent on the median citizen (that is, the citizen who holds the middle ground between the poorest and the richest). In the United States the discrepancy is smaller, but the discrimination is keener. The richest parents, some 10 per cent, can afford private education for their children and help them to benefit from foundation grants. But in addition they obtain ten times per capita amount of public funds if this is compared with the per capita expenditure made on the children of the 10 per cent who are poorest. The principal reasons for this are that the rich children stay longer in school, that a year in a university is disproportionately more expensive than a year in a high school, and that most private universities depend – at least indirectly – on tax-derived finances.

Illich, I.D. op. cit., p. 9.

1. Equal obligatory schooling is economically unfeasible.
2. .... In Latin America 350/1,500 × more public money spent on graduate student than median citizen.
3. .... In US discrimination worse.
4. .... Richest educate children privately.
5. .... Richest obtain 10 × more per capita public money than poorest.
6. .... Rich children longer at school.
7. .... University year more expensive than school year.
8. .... Most private universities depend on tax-derived finances.

Task 6 (Pairs)

Work in pairs.

Student A: Check your notes with another student who has read the same text. Then with the help of the completed notes, explain the argument to your partner, B. Together, discuss how persuasive you find the argument.

Student B: Check your notes with another student who has read the same text. Then with the help of the completed notes, explain the argument to your partner, A. Together, discuss how persuasive you find the argument.

TEXT EXPLORATION

Discourse study: Forms of argument (1)

Task 7 (Individual, then pairs)

Compare these two texts on marriage. They reflect the views of the sociologist, J. Bernard. Underline the main ideas in each text. What differences can you note in the structure of the two arguments? Compare your answers with your partner.

Text 1

Marriage has a beneficial effect on men. Compared to single men of the same age group, married men enjoy better physical and mental health. Their lives are likely to be longer and happier. In addition, they enjoy more successful careers, fill higher status occupations and consequently earn more money. Critics may argue that it is simply that more successful men tend to get married, but the evidence shows that it is marriage which brings about these beneficial effects. Hence the best guarantee of a long, happy, healthy and successful life for a man is to have a wife devoted to homemaking and the care of her husband.

Text 2

Surveys show that more wives than husbands express dissatisfaction with their marriage and consider their marriages unhappy. More wives start divorce proceedings. In addition, wives are much more likely to suffer from stress, anxiety and depression than their partners. Compared to their single peers, wives have poorer physical and mental health. It is clear that for many women, marriage cannot be considered a beneficial experience.

How would you change Text 1 to give it the structure of Text 2? How would you change Text 2 to give it the structure of Text 1?

Text 1 has this structure:

Opinion	*Marriage is beneficial to men.*
Supporting reasons	*Better health.* *Longer, happier lives.* *Better careers.*
Counter-argument dismissed	*Not the case that more successful men marry but that marriage makes men successful.*
Conclusion = opinion restated in stronger terms	*Marriage best guarantee of health, happiness, success for a man.*

Text 2 has this structure:

Evidence	*More wives are unhappy.* *More wives start divorce.* *Wives suffer more stress.* *Single women are healthier.*
Conclusion	*For many women, marriage is not beneficial.*

Both forms of argument are common in texts. Careful reading of the first and last sentences should disclose the main idea. If the idea is not acceptable to you, check the rest of the text for the supporting points.

Paragraphs are often steps in an argument rather than complete arguments. What conclusion could follow from Texts 1 and 2 read as steps in an argument? Compare your answer with the *Key* on page 158.

Grammar and meaning: Even if . . .

'*If*-sentences' may be used to predict the consequences of a proposal. For example:

> If we provided equal schooling for all, poor children could catch up with rich children.

In an argument, they may be used to show what the writer considers are the logical consequences of a statement. For example:

> If we accept that crimes are due to social forces, we should not hold criminals responsible for their actions.

'*Even if*-sentences' may be used to show that proposals will NOT have the expected consequences.

> Even if we provided equal schooling for all, poor children could not catch up with rich children.

They may be used in a counter-argument to show that a statement will NOT have the expected consequences.

> Even if we accept that crimes are due to social forces, we should hold criminals responsible for their actions.

Task 8 (Individual)

Complete these sentences as you consider appropriate.

1. Even if the state provided all requirements,
   a) people would still steal.
   b) people would not steal.
2. a) If divorce was made easier,
   b) Even if divorce was made easier,
   there would be fewer unhappy marriages.
3. a) If housework is to be really valued,
   b) Even if housework is to be really valued,
   husbands should pay their wives for such work.

LIVERPOOL
JOHN MOORES UNIVERSITY
AVRIL ROBARTS LRC
TEL. 0151 231 4022

4. Even if marriage was abolished,
   a) people would still live as families.
   b) people would not live as families.
5. a) If we built more prisons,
   b) Even if we built more prisons,
   we would not solve the problem of increasing crime.
6. Even if the death penalty was reintroduced,
   a) the murder rate would fall.
   b) the murder rate would rise.

Word study: Maximisers and minimisers

Task 9 (Individual, then pairs)

Read this text with and without the words in **bold** type. What effect do these words have? Try to divide them into two sets. Label the sets. Discuss your selection with your partner.

> The traditional approach to parenthood is **completely** unsatisfactory. Women have to spend many hours in child-rearing. Those with professional skills may sacrifice their career **in all respects** for the benefit of **only** one child. Because women spend time caring for their children, the services of many expensively trained teachers, nurses, doctors and other professionals are **altogether** lost to society. Even if child-rearing is shared by the father, it **simply** means that two people waste time on an unproductive task for which they may be **entirely** ill-equipped. Society would be **much** better served if parenthood was made the responsibility of well-trained professional parents who would look after groups of children as a paid occupation. This would end amateur child-rearing and allow the biological parents to **fully** develop their careers for the benefit of society. Critics may argue that children reared in this way would feel rejected, **at least to some extent**, by their natural parents. This is **quite** untrue. Evidence from societies where collective child-rearing is practised shows that children **merely** experience minor upsets and are **hardly** affected by the separation.

Writers try to persuade not only by well-structured argument, but also by well-chosen words. They may try to maximise the points in favour and to minimise the points against their opinion.

APPLICATION

Task 10 (Individual)

Study these statistics (opposite) on divorce in England and Wales. The figures are typical for much of the industrialised world. What reasons can you think of to explain these figures?

2: HOUSEHOLDS AND FAMILIES

2.15 Divorce[1]

	1961	1971	1976	1981	1983	1984	1985	1986	1987	1988
Petitions filed[2] (thousands)										
England & Wales										
By husband	14	44	43	47	45	49	52	50	50	49
By wife	18	67	101	123	124	131	139	131	133	134
Total	32	111	145	170	169	180	191	180	183	183
Decrees nisi granted (thousands)										
England & Wales	27	89	132	148	150	148	162	153	150	155
Decrees absolute granted (thousands)										
England & Wales	25	74	127	146	147	145	160	154	151	153
Scotland	2	5	9	10	13	12	13	13	12	11
Northern Ireland	—	—	1	1	2	2	2	2	2	2
United Kingdom	27	80	136	157	162	158	175	168	165	166
Persons divorcing per thousand married people										
England & Wales	2.1	6.0	10.1	11.9	12.2	12.0	13.4	12.9	12.7	12.8
Percentage of divorces where one or both partners had been divorced in an immediately previous marriage										
England & Wales	*9.3*	*8.8*	*11.6*	*17.1*	*20.0*	*21.0*	*23.0*	*23.2*	*23.5*	*24.0*
Estimated numbers of divorced people who had not remarried (thousands)										
Great Britain										
Men	101	200	405	653	785	847	918	990	1,047	..
Women	184	317	564	890	1,036	1,105	1,178	1,258	1,327	..
Total	285	517	969	1,543	1,821	1,952	2,096	2,248	2,374	..

1 This table includes annulment throughout. See Appendix, Part 2: Divorce.
2 Estimates based on 100 per cent of petitions at the Principal Registry together with a 2 month sample of county court petitions (March and September).

Source: Office of Population Censuses and Surveys; Lord Chancellor's Department

Social Trends, No. 20, 1990, p. 64 (London: Her Majesty's Stationery Office).

Task 11 (Individual)

Read these textbook explanations of the rising divorce statistics. Make brief notes to show the structure of each explanation. Which explanation do you find the most convincing?

Text 1

Nicky Hart argues that the increasing divorce rate can be seen as a 'product of conflict between the changing economic system and its social and ideological superstructure (notably the family)'. In advanced capitalist industrial societies, there is an increasing demand for cheap female wage labour. Wives are encouraged to take up paid employment not only because of the demand for their services, but also because the capitalist controlled media has raised 'material aspirations' – the demand for goods that families desire. These material aspirations can only be satisfied by both spouses working as wage earners. However, conflict results from the contradiction between female wage labour and the normative expectations which surround married life. 'Working wives' are still expected to be primarily responsible for housework and raising children. In addition, they are still expected, to some degree, to play a subservient role to the male head of the household. These normative expectations contradict the wife's role as a wage earner since she is now sharing the economic burden with her husband. Conflict between the spouses can result from this contradiction, and conflict can lead to marital breakdown.

Haralambos, M. (1985) *Sociology, Themes and Perspectives*, 2nd edition, pp. 364–5 (London: Bell & Hyman).

Text 2

As laws and procedures regulating divorce have altered, the divorce rate has tended to increase by leaps and bounds; with each new piece of legislation making divorce more readily available, the rate has risen rapidly for a time before levelling off. Today there is one divorce in Britain for every three marriages. (In the USA the rate is one in two.) Many people have suggested that the higher divorce rates reflect an underlying increase in marital instability; the problem with this argument is that we have no way of knowing how many 'unstable' or 'unhappy' marriages existed before legislation made it possible to dissolve them in a public (and recordable) form. Some commentators have gone further, and argued that more permissive divorce laws in themselves *cause* marital breakdown. But we can certainly be sceptical of such a view, suggesting as it does that happily married couples can suddenly be persuaded to abandon their relationship, propelled by the attraction of a new divorce law. A more plausible explanation for rises in the divorce rate after the passage of a law is that unhappily married couples were for the first time given access to a legal solution to pre-existent marital problems; in other words, changes in divorce laws are less likely to cause marital breakdown than to provide new types of solution where breakdown has already occurred.

Bilton, T. et al. (1987) *Introductory Sociology*, 2nd edition, p. 301 (London: Macmillan).

Unit 9 Work

The end point of studies for most students is work. Attitudes to work create friction or harmony in the workplace. The wealth of a nation depends on work. With the introduction of new technology, the future of work is changing. In this unit we will read about work in texts from Industrial Psychology, Labour Relations, Economics and Business Studies.

This unit aims to develop the reading skills required for:

1. comparing viewpoints
2. detecting false forms of argument
3. understanding how writers emphasise and distance themselves from viewpoints

TO MAKE YOU THINK

Task 1 (Individual, then pairs)

Write down as many words associated with WORK as you can think of in one minute. Compare your list with your neighbour. Then try to group your words into categories, for example, 'Rewards of work'.

Task 2 (Individual)

You are going to read a text about work. Before you read, note your own views on these aspects of work.

	Your views
NATURE OF WORK What is work?	
EFFECT OF WORKING CONDITIONS How do working conditions affect workers' attitudes?	
MOTIVATION FOR WORK Why do people work?	

Task 3 (Pairs)

Work in pairs, A and B.

Student A: Read Text 1. Note briefly in your section of the table the 'orthodox' view on the three aspects of work listed in the text.

Student B: Read Text 2. Note briefly in your section of the table the author's view on the three aspects of work listed in the text.

	Text 1	*Text 2*
NATURE OF WORK		
EFFECT OF WORKING CONDITIONS		
MOTIVATION FOR WORK		

Text 1 'Orthodox' view

THE orthodox view of work which has been accepted by most managers and industrial psychologists is a simple one, and fifty years of industrial psychology and more than a century of managerial practice have been founded upon it. Regarding the *nature* of work, the orthodox view accepts the Old Testament belief that physical labour is a curse imposed on man as a punishment for his sins and that the sensible man labours solely in order to keep himself and his family alive, or, if he is fortunate, in order to make a sufficient surplus to enable him to do the things he really likes.* Regarding the *conditions* of work, it is assumed that improving the conditions of the job will cause the worker's natural dislike of it to be somewhat mitigated, and, in addition, will keep him physically healthy and therefore more efficient in the mechanistic sense. Finally, regarding the *motivation* of work, the carrot and stick hypothesis asserts that the main positive incentive is money, the main negative one fear of unemployment.

Brown, J.A.C. (1954) *The Social Psychology of Industry*, p. 186 (London: Penguin).

Text 2 Author's view

(1) Work is an essential part of a man's life since it is that aspect of his life which gives him status and binds him to society. Ordinarily men and women like their work, and at most periods of history always have done so. When they do not like it, the fault lies in the psychological and social conditions of the job rather than in the worker. Furthermore, work is a *social* activity.

(2) The morale of the worker (i.e. whether or not he works willingly) has no *direct* relationship whatsoever to the material conditions of the job. Investigations into temperature, lighting, time and motion study, noise, and humidity have not the slightest bearing on morale, although they may have a bearing on physical health and comfort.

(3) There are many incentives, of which, under normal conditions, money is one of the least important. Unemployment is a powerful negative incentive, precisely because (1) is true. That is to say, unemployment is feared because it cuts man off from his society.

Brown, J.A.C. op cit., p. 187.

Task 4 (Pairs)

Find out from your partner the views expressed in his or her text. Note them in the appropriate section of the table in Task 3.

Now read each other's text to check if anything has been missed out.

Task 5 (Groups)

Work in groups. Discuss your own views and those expressed in the texts. Do you agree with either text? Have your views changed through reading the texts?

READING AND INTERACTION

Critical reading: Comparing viewpoints

In Unit 8 we studied how to break down an argument into points. When comparing different viewpoints, we can proceed in the same way, then compare the arguments point by point. Before doing this, it is useful to be clear about your own opinions on the topic so that you do not simply absorb what you read but react to the writer's views. You can then argue with the text, deciding whether to accept or reject each idea or to wait for further evidence before deciding.

A useful tool in comparing viewpoints is to make a summary of each text.

Task 6 (Individual, then groups)

The texts in this section are about solutions to unemployment. Before you read, note some possible solutions to unemployment. Discuss your proposals with others in your group. Try to decide on the best solution.

For the next three tasks, work in groups, A and B.

Group A: Do Tasks 7, 8 and 9.
Group B: Do Tasks 10, 11 and 12.

Task 7 (Group A)

Read Text 1 and complete the summary which follows. When you have finished, compare your summary with another student from your group.

Text 1

One argument used to support the idea that employment will continue to be the dominant form of work, and that employment will eventually become available for all who want it, is that working time will continue to fall. People in jobs will work fewer hours in the day, fewer days in the week, fewer weeks in the year, and fewer years in a lifetime, than they do now. This will mean that more jobs will be available for more people. This, it is said, is the way we should set about restoring full employment.

There is no doubt that something of this kind will happen. The shorter working week, longer holidays, earlier retirement, more sabbaticals, job-sharing – these and other ways of reducing the amount of time people spend on their jobs – are certainly likely to spread. A mix of part-time paid work and part-time unpaid work is likely to become a much more common work pattern than today, and a flexi-life pattern of work – involving paid employment at certain stages of life, but not at others – will become widespread. But it is surely unrealistic to assume that this will make it possible to restore full employment as the dominant form of work.

In the first place, so long as employment remains the overwhelmingly important form of work and source of income for most people that it is today, it is very difficult to see how reductions in employees' working time can take place on a scale sufficiently large and at a pace sufficiently fast to make it possible to share out the available paid employment to everyone who wants it. Such negotiations as there have recently been, for example in Britain and Germany, about the possibility of introducing a 35-hour working week, have highlighted some of the difficulties. But, secondly, if changes of this kind were to take place at a pace and on a scale sufficient to make it possible to share employment among all who wanted it, the resulting situation – in which most people would not be working in their jobs for more than two or three short days a week – could hardly continue to be one in which employment was still regarded as the only truly valid form of work. There would be so many people spending so much of their time on other activities, including other forms of useful work, that the primacy of employment would be bound to be called into question, at least to some extent.

Robertson, J. (1985) *Future Work: Jobs, self-employment and leisure after the Industrial Age*, pp. 23–4 (London: Gower/Maurice Temple Smith).

This paragraph summarises the main argument of the text. Try to complete the blanks. The line numbers will help you find the points you need.

	lines
If working time falls, then .... The result will be	4–7
.... Working time will fall because of ....,	9–13
longer holidays, earlier retirement, more sabbaticals and	
.... This means a mix of part-time paid and part-	
time unpaid work will become more common but	17–19
.... The first reason is that the reduction of working	
time cannot take place on a scale and at a pace sufficient to	24–26
.... The second reason is that if ...., it	29–31
would create a situation where full employment would no	
longer be the main form of work.	

Task 8 (Group A)

Here are the steps which make up the argument in the text. Try to complete them. When you have finished, compare your answers with another student from your group.

		lines
1. IF working time falls THEN		4–6
2. THEREFORE		6–7
3. Working time will fall BECAUSE OF	....	10–11
4.	longer holidays	
5.	....	
6.	more sabbaticals	
7. AND	....	
8. THEREFORE		13–17
9. BUT		17–19
10. BECAUSE the scale and pace are insufficient		
11. and BECAUSE IF .... THEN full employment would no longer be the only form of work		29–31

Task 9 (Group A)

Consider each step (1 to 11) in the argument. Then decide whether you accept, reject or require further evidence for each step.

Task 10 (Group B)

Read Text 2 and complete the summary which follows. When you have finished, compare your summary with another student from your group.

Text 2

There is an apparently simple solution to mass unemployment: the shortening of working hours by 10, 15 or 20%. For several reasons such simplicity is more apparent than real. Given the comparatively low level of British wages and salaries, organised labour would not and could not accept wage cuts by the same proportion. Any attempt to create employment for all by such cuts might create social upheaval on a scale larger than that of riots. To pay the same wages for significantly reduced hours to a larger workforce, however, would lower British competitiveness on the world market even further. But even if the world market could absorb more expensive goods – an unlikely assumption anyhow – the attempt could not succeed because of the geographical distribution of unemployment and the mismatch between the skills of the unemployed and the skills required by modern enterprises.

And yet, in the long run the shortening of working hours per day, per year or per lifetime is the most constructive measure if new technologies actually reduce the amount of work required to give the population a respectable standard of living. The psychological benefits of employment are not tied to an eight-hour day or a 40-hour week. They would accrue even in the improbable case for this century that working hours could be halved without lowering the standard of living. In this country as elsewhere a gradual reduction of working hours is actually taking place and there are efforts afoot to cut overtime, one of the few positive aspects of an otherwise dark picture. The immediate impact of such developments will be mostly an improvement in the quality of working life for the employed; it is inevitably a slow way of reducing the number of the unemployed.

Jahoda, M. (1982) *Employment and Unemployment*, pp. 98–9 (Cambridge: Cambridge University Press).

This paragraph summarises the main argument of the text. Try to complete the blanks. The line numbers will help you find the points you need.

	lines
It may seem that if working hours are cut by 10 to 20%, then	
.... But labour will not accept wage cuts on such a	1–2
scale. If wage cuts are imposed, ... If hours are cut	5–7
but wages maintained, Britain will be unable to compete in	
world markets because her goods will be so expensive. Even if	
Britain's goods could be sold, unemployment would not fall	
because of .... and the mismatch between the skills	11–12
the unemployed can offer and the skills required for modern	
employment.	
Shortening working hours has value because	17–18
from employment even when we work less. Cutting hours will	
improve the quality of working life for the employed but	
....	25–26

Task 11 (Group B)

Here are the steps which make up the argument in the text. Try to complete them. When you have finished, compare your answers with another student from your group.

	lines
1. IF working hours are cut THEN	1–2
2. BUT labour will not accept wage cuts on such a scale	
3. IF .... THEN there will be serious social upheaval	5–7
4. IF .... THEN Britain will be unable to compete in world markets	7–9

5. BECAUSE her goods will be so expensive
6. IF Britain's goods could be sold THEN 11
7. BECAUSE OF its geographical distribution
8. AND................. 12–13
9. ....BECAUSE we get the psychological benefits of work even when we work less 14–17
10. THEREFORE cutting working hours will improve the quality of life for the employed
11. BUT 25–26

Task 12 (Group B)

Consider each step (1 to 11) in the argument. Then decide whether you accept, reject or require further evidence for each step.

Task 13 (Groups A and B)

Work with a student from the other group. Explain the argument in your text to him or her and give your own reaction to that argument. Listen to his or her explanation and note the points of agreement and disagreement between the texts. Which argument do you find the most convincing?

TEXT EXPLORATION

Discourse study: Forms of argument (2)

In Unit 8 we studied two forms of argument. Here, to sharpen your critical reading abilities, we will study some false forms of argument you may meet.

Task 14 (Individual, then pairs)

Read the following texts carefully. Think about the argument presented in each text. Does the argument convince you that the writer's conclusion is justified?

Text 1

Women are more likely to strike than men because they take a more emotional attitude to problems at work. The majority of workers in the clothing industry are female. Hence labour disputes are a common feature in factories which produce garments.

Text 2

The 1920s in Western Europe were a period of high unemployment. In the late 20s and early 30s extreme right-wing political parties developed in Germany, Spain, Portugal and Italy. It seems obvious, therefore, that unemployment leads to the rise of fascism.

Text 3

Much of the success of Japanese industry is due to the way in which management and workers are treated as equal partners. There is no gap between white collar and blue collar workers. Both share the same canteens and there is only one entrance for all employees. If these measures were adopted in our country there would be much less industrial friction.

Text 4

Japan and Switzerland are both countries with few natural resources. Like Japan, Switzerland imports much of its fuel and almost all of its raw materials. Both countries base their economies on the production of high-quality, high-value goods like watches and machine tools. Like Japan therefore, Switzerland should have few labour problems.

Text 5

As Marx states, labour creates wealth and this wealth is divided between capitalist and worker. If wages rise, profits fall and if wages fall, profits will rise. Hence capitalists everywhere seek to keep wages at as low a level as possible so that they can maximise their share of the wealth.

Text 6

During the strike of power workers in the UK in 1975, factories were only able to operate for three days per week instead of the usual five. Nevertheless, productivity showed little change. This evidence shows that manufacturers have nothing to fear from reducing the working week by 40%.

Text 7

Workers who do boring, repetitive tasks, like assembly-line workers, are more likely to strike than those who have varied and interesting work like craftsmen. Requiring workers to do the same thing, day in, day out, is likely, therefore, to lead to strikes.

Word study: Emphasising and distancing

Task 15 (Pairs)

Study these extracts from texts used in this unit. Why has the writer included the words in **bold** type? Try reading the texts without the words in **bold** type; then with the words in **bold**.

1. The morale of the worker has no direct relationship **whatsoever** to the material conditions of the job. Investigations into temperature, lighting, time and motion study, noise and humidity have not **the slightest** bearing on morale.
2. This, **it is said,** is the way we should set about restoring full employment.
3. **There is no doubt that** something of this kind will happen.

LIVERPOOL
JOHN MOORES UNIVERSITY
AVRIL ROBARTS LRC
TEL. 0151 231 4022

4. But it is **surely** unrealistic to assume that this will make it possible to restore full employment as the dominant form of work.
5. There would be so many people spending so much of their time on other activities, including other forms of useful work, that the primacy of unemployment would be **bound to be** called into question, at least to some extent.
6. There is an **apparently** simple solution to mass unemployment: the shortening of working hours by 10, 15 or 20%.

Writers may try to convince their readers by adding words to emphasise their message. In Unit 8 we studied how maximisers could be used in this way. Writers may also try to distance themselves from statements which they do not agree with or are not completely confident about. Which of the phrases above were included to emphasise and which to distance?

Study these ways in which writers may emphasise this message:

Employers should ensure that the views of the workforce are represented in the boardroom.

1. Choice of modal verb:
   Employers **must** *ensure that the views of the workforce are represented in the boardroom.*
2. Using a maximiser – often an adverbial:
   Clearly *employers should ensure that the views of the workforce are represented in the boardroom.*
3. Changing the structure:
   What employers should ensure is *that the views of the workforce are represented in the boardroom.*
4. Repetition by rephrasing:
   Employers should ensure that the views of the workforce are represented in the boardroom. **In other words** *they should appoint worker directors.*

APPLICATION

Task 16 (Individual)

What are your views on the future of work in your society? Think of these points:

Will there be full employment?
Who will work?
Where will people work?
What will work consist of?

Note your views before reading further.

Task 17 (Individual)

Answer each of the in-text questions before going on to the next section of text.

Leisure in place of work – A realistic goal?

1. What will the text be about?
2. What do you think is the writer's attitude to his topic?

The idea that in a post-employment society employment could be largely replaced by leisure activities and that increasing numbers of people could live lives of leisure, is open to serious question from two points of view.

3. What arguments do you think the writer will use?

First, many people without employment would resist the idea that they were expected to make no useful contribution, either towards meeting their own needs or towards meeting those of other people, and were merely expected to keep themselves amused and out of trouble. They would resent the sense of uselessness and futility which this would imply, and feel that their lives were condemned to be empty of value and meaning. It is not as if most of us today are heirs to an aristocratic tradition of cultured leisure. We have inherited the protestant work ethic, and the need to feel useful which goes with it.

4. Break the argument in lines 5–14 into steps and note them. Which steps do you accept?
5. Do the same for the argument in lines 15–22.

Second, many of the people still in employment would resent the idea that they were expected to support large numbers of idle drones. The situation would be one in which the employed were perceived as doing all the useful work and the unemployed were seen, on a larger scale and a more permanent basis than today, as making no useful contribution to society. The question of how to finance the leisure of the unemployed in a leisure society would thus be a difficult one.

6. Explain why this would be difficult.

They would need a money income. Thus some extension of today's unemployment and social security benefits systems would be needed, perhaps going as far as the introduction of a Guaranteed Basic Income (GBI).

7. What do you think a GBI would be?

But this would be much more difficult to introduce in the context of a society clearly split between workers and non-workers, than in the context of a society in which it was understood that the purpose of the basic income was to give all citizens the freedom to choose their own mix of paid and unpaid work.

8. Is it possible to say what kind of society the writer would like?
9. Explain why the writer has used the words in **bold** type.

Finally, if anything resembling the leisure society **did come** about, **one thing is sure**. Many of those at leisure would **in fact** use their time for useful activities of many kinds. **In other words**, they would find ways of working on their own account, to provide useful goods and services for themselves and for one another. A leisure society would automatically transform itself, **at least to some extent**, into an ownwork society.

10. What will the writer's conclusion be?

In short, the prospect of moving towards a leisure society cannot be accepted as providing a realistic solution to the present crisis of unemployment and work.

11. Do you share his conclusion?

Robertson, J. op. cit., pp. 24–5.

PART 3 THE TOOLS OF RESEARCH

Unit 10 Using reference sources (1)

Often we can't find all the information we need in our textbooks. We have to consult other sources to find the extra information we require. It may also help our understanding of a particular topic to refer to a book which takes a different approach from that of our textbook. For essays, assignments and dissertations we have to demonstrate that we have consulted a range of sources and taken different viewpoints into account. In these circumstances, it is important that we can locate quickly the best sources for our purposes.

In this unit we will consider the kinds of help that different reference sources can provide. We will focus on the reading skills which allow us to use these sources effectively.

TO MAKE YOU THINK

Task 1 (Individual)

Where would you look for help with these problems?

1. The title of Humphrey Bogart's last film.
2. The location of Mpwapwa.
3. The most recent figures for the amount of rice produced by major rice exporters.
4. The difference between the behaviourist and the cognitive view of language learning.
5. A list of books about the education of women.
6. The main political parties in India.
7. Who was W.K. Kellogg?
8. Which spelling is correct – 'enrolment' or 'enrollment'?
9. The difference between RAM and ROM in computing.

Task 2 (Individual)

What sort of information would you expect to find in these reference books?

1. *Chambers Technical Dictionary*
2. *Encyclopaedia Britannica*
3. *Longman Dictionary of Contemporary English*
4. *The Statesman's Year Book*
5. *Work on Women: A guide to the literature*
6. *The Cambridge Encyclopedia of Language*
7. *UN Monthly bulletin of statistics*
8. *Encyclopedia Americana*
9. *The Times Index-Gazeteer of the World*
10. *Webster's Biographical Dictionary*

Task 3 (Individual)

Which of the books listed in Task 2 could help you with the problems in Task 1?

LOCATING SPECIFIC INFORMATION

Task 4 (Individual)

Try to find the answers to these questions in this encyclopaedia entry as quickly as you can. Warning! You will not be able to find the answers to all of these questions. No reference source can contain all information on a particular topic. Knowing when it is time to give up and try another source is important.

1. When was breakfast cereal first developed?
2. Who invented breakfast cereal?
3. What types of breakfast cereal exist?
4. At what stage in the process are vitamins added?
5. Why did the sale of breakfast cereals increase dramatically from the 1950s?
6. Which manufacturer has the biggest share of the breakfast cereal market?
7. Most breakfast cereals are directed towards what section of the market?

breakfast cereal, grain food, usually precooked or ready-to-eat, that is customarily eaten with milk or cream for breakfast in the United States and elsewhere, often sweetened with sugar, syrup, or fruit. The modern commercial concept of cereal food originated in the vegetarian beliefs of the American Seventh-day Adventists, who in the 1860s formed the Western Health Reform Institute, later renamed the Battle Creek Sanitarium, in Battle Creek, Mich. The entrepreneurial possibilities of the ground, thin-baked cereal dough served to the Sanitarium's patients inspired two men, C.W. Post and W.K. Kellogg, each to found his own business. In the late 20th century the ready-to-eat breakfast cereal industry sold the equivalent of several billion bowls of cereal to Americans yearly, having far surpassed the market for the traditional "hot" cereals made from rolled oatmeal or enriched wheat farina.

Ready-to-eat breakfast cereals are of four basic types: flaked, made from corn, wheat, or rice that has been broken down into grits, cooked with flavours and syrups, and then pressed into flakes between cooled rollers; puffed, made by exploding cooked wheat or rice from a pressure chamber, thus expanding the grain to several times its original size; shredded, made from pressure-cooked wheat that is squeezed into strands by heavy rollers, then cut into biscuits and dried; and granular, made by a process in which a stiff dough made from wheat and malted barley flour, salt, yeast, and water is fermented, baked thoroughly, and then, after being crumbled and rebaked, is ground into rough grains. As a final step in each process, the cereal is treated to restore vitamins lost through cooking and often coated with sweet flavouring.

Until the mid- to late 1950s, the market for ready-to-eat breakfast cereal was relatively small, making its subsequent rapid growth one of the most dramatic success stories in modern advertising. By skillful product diversification and promotion, ready-to-eat products took over the breakfast food market—children found a prize in every package or associated a cereal with their favourite cartoon characters, while their parents, ever reminded of the convenience and the nutritional value of fortified cereals, could enter manufacturer-sponsored contests for prizes of their own. Late in the century, the majority of breakfast cereals continued to be directed toward the children's market, with entertainment-oriented packaging and a wide variety of "treat" flavours. Alongside these, the so-called health food movement fostered, or revived, cereals composed of "natural" whole grain and fruit in the old-fashioned granola style.

Encyclopaedia Britannica (1986) Micropaedia, Vol. 2, p. 491 (Chicago: Encyclopaedia Britannica Inc.).

Task 5 (Pairs)

Write six questions on this dictionary entry to test your partner's speed at locating specific information. Make sure you know what the right answers are. Time how long it takes your partner to find the right answers. Then try your partner's questions in the same way.

If you are working alone, refer to the *Key*. It contains six questions for you to try.

radiocarbon dating. In ARCHAEOLOGY, a method of DATING pioneered by W.F. Libby, who first proposed it in 1946. It is based on the rate of decay of the radioactive (see RADIOACTIVITY) ISOTOPE C^{14} incorporated in organic matter. C^{14} is produced from nitrogen^{14} by cosmic RADIATION in the upper atmosphere and is absorbed by living matter in the form of carbon dioxide. The proportion of C^{12} to C^{14} remains constant in the atmosphere and in living plants and animals, but as soon as the organism dies, and further absorption of carbon dioxide ceases, the proportion of C^{14} to C^{12} is steadily decreased by the decay of the unstable radioactive isotope. If we know the HALF-LIFE of C^{14} and the ratio of C^{14} to C^{12} in a sample it is, in theory, possible to work out the absolute age at time of death for a substance which was once alive. The validity of the method as an absolute dating technique rests on two basic assumptions: that the half-life of C^{14} can be accurately determined, and that C^{14} has been produced at a constant rate. Early calculations used a half-life of 5,568 ± 30 years (the 'old half-life'), but recent recalculation suggests that 5,730 is a better approximation (the 'preferred half-life'). Comparison between radiocarbon dates and historical dates (e.g. obtained from dating Egyptian woodwork) has for some time shown a certain lack of CORRELATION. Recent studies involving the radiocarbon dating of tree rings of known age (see under DENDROCHRONOLOGY) have confirmed the discrepancy. It is now suggested that the production of C^{14} was not constant throughout time and that it is necessary to recalibrate 'radiocarbon years' against tree-ring dates to arrive at 'real years'.

Dates are always quoted ± x years, representing the standard statistical error. 4300 ± 50 B.C. means that there is a 2:1 chance of the date lying between 4250 and 4350. Dates are often published B.P. (before the present), the present being 1950. In the wake of the confusion following the apparent need to recalibrate, some writers have adopted the procedure of quoting the date 'b.c.' meaning 'radiocarbon years' and offering a recalibrated date 'B.C.' to represent an approximation to 'real years'. Each data assessment is uniquely numbered according to international agreement. It is accepted that this laboratory number should always be quoted. B.C.

Bibl: T. Watkins, *Radiocarbon: Calibration and Prehistory* (Edinburgh, 1975).

Bullock, A., Stallybrass, O. and Trombley, S. eds (1988) *The Fontana Dictionary of Modern Thought*, p. 717 (London: Fontana).

Task 6 (Individual)

Study the table of rice production on page 118. Locate this information as quickly as you can.

1. Name the three largest rice producers.
2. Which country has the highest productivity (greatest yield per hectare)? Estimate.
3. Rank these countries in terms of rice production: Burma, Nepal, Japan, Bangladesh.
4. What general statement can you make about rice production in Bangladesh between 1985 and 1988?
5. Using the table as evidence, give one possible reason for the decline in Mexican rice production between 1985 and 1988.
6. What problem is there in calculating the productivity of Vietnam with regard to rice?

RICE (Paddy)

Countries	Area (1,000 hectares) Average 1979-81	1985	1986	1987	1988	Production (1,000 tonnes) Average 1979–81	1985	1986	1987	1988
Bangladesh	10,310	10,399	10,610	10,322	10,000	20,125	22,562	23,110	23,120	21,900
Brazil	5,932	4,755	5,585	6,000	5,961	8,533	9,027	10,374	10,425	11,804
Burma	4,684	4,661	4,666	4,641	4,715	12,637	14,317	14,126	13,722	14,000
Cambodia	1,186	1,750	1,700	1,546	1,600	1,160	2,100	2,000	1,855	2,000
China	34,323	32,634	32,798	32,694	32,500	145,665	171,416	174,790	176,958	172,365
Colombia	428	386	325	385	389	1,831	1,798	1,521	1,865	1,775
Egypt	416	389	423	412	330*	2,376	2,311	2,445	2,279	1,900*
India	40,091	41,137	41,167	38,319	41,000	74,557	95,818	90,779	84,538	101,950
Indonesia	9,063	9,902	9,988	9,923	10,090	29,570	39,033	39,727	40,078	41,769
Iran	433	480	489	510	482	1,448	1,775	1,828	1,920	1,757*
Italy	176	186	192	190	198	989	1,123	1,137	1,064	1,094
Japan	2,384	2,342	2,303	2,146	2,132*	13,320	14,578	14,559	13,284	12,419
Korea, North	793	840	860	875	885	4,970	5,800	6,000	6,200	6,350
Korea, South	1,230	1,237	1,236	1,262	1,260	6,780	7,855	7,872	7,596	8,400*
Madagascar	1,182	1,181	1,188	1,214	1,200	2,055	2,178	2,230	2,296	2,100
Malaysia	658	656	628	641	630	2,053	1,953	1,745	1,697	1,669
Mexico	153	220	158	155	120*	528	809	545	591	420*
Nepal	1,275	1,391	1,333	1,423	1,400	2,361	2,804	2,372	2,982	2,787
Nigeria	517	700*	720*	730*	650	1,027	1,515*	1,416	1,450*	1,400
Pakistan	1,981	1,863	2,066	1,963	1,939	4,884	4,378	5,230	4,861	4,577
Philippines	3,513	3,306	3,464	3,256	3,293	7,893	8,806	9,247	8,540	8,971
Sri Lanka	819	867	836	679	811	2,093	2,661	2,588	2,128	2,466
Thailand	8,953	9,833	9,194	9,083	10,417	16,967	20,264	18,868	18,042	20,813
USSR	637	671	621	657	660	2,558	2,572	2,633	2,683	2,900
USA	1,345	1,009	955	944	1,172	6,968	6,120	6,049	5,879	7,237
Vietnam	5,558	5,704	5,689	5,594	5,600	11,663	15,875	16,003	15,103	15,200*
World total	145,602	144,493	145,157	141,497	145,602	396,290	472,714	472,482	464,514	483,466

*Unofficial figures.

The Statesman's Year Book 1990/91, 127th edition, p. xx (London: Macmillan).

7. What conclusion can you make from the world totals for area and production for the period covered by the table?

CHOOSING THE BEST SOURCE

Task 7 (Individual)

If you wish to read more about a subject, how can you obtain suggestions for further reading?

Which of these suggestions from students would be helpful in your situation?

1. Ask your tutor for a reading list.
2. Use your textbook. You may find a recommended reading list after each chapter or at the end of the book.
3. Look up the topic in an encyclopaedia. The entry may give a bibliography for further reading.
4. Look for a specialist bibliography in your library.
5. If your library catalogue is on-line, conduct a subject search.
6. Check the library shelves for titles with the same shelf number as a textbook you know in this area.

Task 8 (Individual, then groups)

Study this list of books on study skills from a university library on-line catalogue. Select from it books which might help you to improve your skills in reading textbooks.

Compare your selection with your neighbours. Try to agree on a list of not more than three books which may be worth referring to. Discuss the factors which influenced your choice.

```
     Adler (Mortimer Jerome)
HOW TO READ A BOOK; A GUIDE TO SELF-EDUCATION
  8. Lond (1940)                        .028 Adl
-----------------------------------------------------
     Barrass, Robert
STUDY!: A GUIDE TO EFFECTIVE STUDY, REVISION AND
EXAMINATION TECHNIQUES
London, Chapman and Hall, 1984         .028 Bar
-----------------------------------------------------
     Ellis (Richard) and Hopk (Konrad)
HOW TO SUCCEED IN WRITTEN WORK AND STUDY
London, Collins, 1985                   .028 Ell
-----------------------------------------------------
     Houle (Cyril Orvin)
CONTINUING YOUR EDUCATION
New York, 1964                          .028 Hou
-----------------------------------------------------
HOW TO READ A BOOK IN THE BEST WAY By a Wrangler.
Lond., 1860                             S.B. .504/J
-----------------------------------------------------
```

Joint Industry Committee for National Readership Surveys
NATIONAL READERSHIP SURVEY 1968-70
Lond. Stat. Ref. .028 Joi

Klein (Marion H.)
DYNAMICS OF COMPREHENSION; HOW TO LEARN FROM A COLLEGE TEXTBOOK
New York, 1970 .028 Kle

Main (Alexander N.)
ENCOURAGING EFFECTIVE LEARNING; AN APPROACH TO STUDY COUNSELLING
Edin., 1980 .028 Mai

Meenes (Max)
STUDYING AND LEARNING 8th pr. (Random House Papers in Psychol. p.p. 9)
New York, 1967 P.028 Mee

Millman (Jason) and Pank (Walter)
HOW TO TAKE TESTS (McGraw-Hill Paperbacks)
New York, copyright 1969 .028 Mil

Open University
PREPARING TO STUDY (By M.E. Richardson and others)
Milton Keynes, 1979 F.028 Ope

Palmer (Richard) and Pope (Chris)
BRAIN TRAIN: STUDYING FOR SUCCESS
London, Spon, 1984 .028 Pal

Richards (Ivor Armstrong)
HOW TO READ A PAGE: A COURSE IN EFFECTIVE READING WITH AN INTRODUCTION TO A HUNDRED GREAT WORDS
Lond., 1954 .028 Ric

Sargant (Edmund Beale) and Whishaw (Bernhard) Eds
A GUIDE BOOK TO BOOKS
Lond., 1891 O.S..028 Sar

Savage (Ernest Albert)
A LIBRARIAN LOOKS AT READERS: OBSERVATION FOR BOOK SELECTION AND PERSONAL SERVICE
Lond., 1947 .028 Sav

Stavely (Ronald)
NOTES ON SOME PROBLEMS IN READING (Lond. Sch. of Lib. and Archives, Occas. Publ. No. 4)
School of Librarianship and Archives, 1954
.028 Sta

Task 9 (Individual)

In the text above, the dates of publication help you to know whether the book will be of value, but you must rely mainly on the titles to predict how useful the text may be. Some reading lists and some on-line catalogues provide only brief titles. What topics do you predict these textbooks will cover?

1. *Encouraging Effective Learning*
2. *The Essential Left*
3. *Workless*
4. *Doing Your Research Project*
5. *Brain train*
6. *Mothers Alone*
7. *Earth, Water, Wind and Sun*

Task 10 (Individual)

Each of the textbooks in Task 9 has a subtitle. Try to match each brief title with its subtitle.

How accurate were your predictions in Task 9 about the topics covered by these books?

a) *A Guide for First-Time Researchers in Education and Social Science*
b) *Four Classic Texts on the Principles of Socialism*
c) *Poverty and the Fatherless Family*
d) *Some Unemployed Men and Their Families*
e) *An approach to study counselling*
f) *Studying for success*
g) *Our energy alternatives*

Task 11 (Individual)

For many subjects, there are bibliographies which list sources for different topics. The amount of information provided in bibliographies varies. Study this list of texts on the topic of Education for Women taken from a bibliography of writing about women.

Select a suitable source or suitable sources for each of these study areas:

1. Women in higher education in the UK
2. Women and science education
3. Secondary School education for girls
4. Educating the sexes separately
5. Female students in US colleges

BAKER, L. *The Seven Sisters and the Failure of Women's Education* (Macmillan, New York, 1976).

BLACKSTONE, T. The Education of Girls Today, in A. Oakley and J. Mitchell (eds.) *The Rights and Wrongs of Women* (Penguin, Harmondsworth, 1976) .

BORING, P. Sex Stereotyping in Educational Guidance, in *Sex Role Stereotyping in the Schools* (National Educational Association, Washington, D.C., 1973).

BRIERLEY, J. Sex Differences in Education (*Trends in Education* February, 1975).

BRITTAIN, V. *Women at Oxford* (Harrap, London, 1960).

BYRNE, E. *Women and Education* (Tavistock, London, 1978).

DEEM, R. *Women and Schooling* (Routledge and Kegan Paul, London, 1978).

DEPARTMENT OF EDUCATION AND SCIENCE *Curricula Differences between the Sexes* (Education Survey 21, HMSO, London, 1975).

FRAZIER, N. and SADKER, M. *Sexism in Schools and Society* (Harper and Row, New York, 1973).

GRAHAM, P. Expansion and Exclusion: A History of Women in American Higher Education, (*Signs* **3**, (4) Spring 1978).

KAMM, J. *How Different from Us: A Biography of Miss Buss and Miss Beale* (Methuen, London, 1958).

LEVY, B. Sex Role Socialisation in the Schools, in, *Sex Role Stereotyping in the Schools* (National Educational Association, Washington, D.C., 1973).

MARKS, P. Femininity in the Classroom: An Account of Changing Attitudes, in A. Oakley and J. Mitchell (eds.) *The Rights and Wrongs of Women* (Penguin, Harmondsworth, 1976).

NEWCOMER, M. *A Century of Higher Education for Women* (Harper and Row, New York, 1959).

OATES, M. and WILLIAMSON, S. Women's Colleges and Women Achievers (*Signs* **3** (4) Spring, 1978).

ROBY, P. Women and American Higher Education (*Annals of the American Academy of Political and Social Science* **404** 1972).

SHAW, J. Finishing School: Some Implications of Sex Segregated Education, in, D. Barker and S. Allen (eds.) *Sexual Divisions and Society: Process and Change* (Tavistock, London, 1976).

SHARPE, S. *Just Like a Girl* (Penguin, Hardmondsworth, 1976).

SIGNS *Women, Science and Society* (Special Issue: **4** (1) Autumn 1978).

UNESCO *Women, Education, Equality: A Decade of Experiment* (UNESCO Press, Paris, 1975).

WOLPE, A. *Some Processes in Sexist Education* (Women's Research and Resources Centre, Explorations in Feminism, London, 1976).

Evans, M. and Morgan, D. (1979) *Work on Women*, pp. 30–3 (London: Tavistock Publications).

Choosing sources from a bibliography requires a mixture of skills – scanning, predicting and evaluating. When you evaluate a source from the information given in a bibliography, you judge how useful it will be in meeting your study needs. The more information given in the bibliography, the easier it is to evaluate the source. Annotated bibliographies provide comments on each source. In the next task, note how the comments on each title help you make the right choice.

Task 12 (Individual)

Using this extract from an annotated bibliography, choose the best atlas for the following study needs. Note only the number of the relevant atlas, i.e. C656–C670. Work as quickly as you can.

1. Growth of the United States, 1775–1853
2. Maps of the stars
3. Location of a number of small towns in East Africa
4. Pronunciation of Tbilisi, Baluchistan and Antakya
5. Map of the Pacific
6. Street plan of Tokyo
7. Population of major South American cities
8. Detailed maps of Germany before re-unification

ATLASES

General-Reference Large World Atlases

C656 The Times atlas of the world, comprehensive edition. 6th ed. London: Times Books, 1980. 123 plates; 227p. (first pub. 1955–59, in 5v.; 1v. ed. first pub. 1967)

The outstanding general-reference large-format world atlas. Excellent cartography. Physical-political maps show locations and relief. Thematic maps. Gazetteer (see C625) has more than 200,000 place names, with map location and latitude and longitude.

C657 Rand McNally and Co. The new international atlas. Chicago: Rand McNally, 1984. 320p. of maps and text; 231p. index and tables. (updated reprinting of 1980 ed.; 1st ed. 1969.)

A major, high-quality general-reference world atlas based on international collaboration in editing and production, with text in English, German, Spanish, and French. To facilitate comparison among areas, only four scales are used on regional maps: 1:12,000,000, 1:6,000,000, 1:3,000,000, and 1:1,000,000. Special maps of the world's major urban areas are scaled at 1:300,000. Primarily physical-political maps, with relief shown by shading. Index has about 160,000 names and indicates map location and latitude and longitude. Includes glossary of geographical terms, world information table, and population of cities and towns.

C658 Britannica atlas. Chicago: Encyclopaedia Britannica, 1979. 312p.; 222p. index. (Present ed. basically from 1969)

Basic maps the same as in Rand McNally *International atlas.* Feature of special interest is the "World scene" (p.283–320), with thematic maps of political, cultural, economic, and physical phenomena.

C659 Hammond, Inc. Hammond medallion world atlas. New census ed. Maplewood, N.J.: Hammond, 1982. Various paging. [672p.]

World and regional maps. Special features: (1) combines maps, index, and statistical data on each double-page layout: (2) political subdivisions of each country are shown. A complex assemblage of basic political maps supplemented by many smaller maps of physical features, economic characteristics, and special maps. Master index of more than 100,000 names. Includes separately paged sections: atlas of Bible lands (32p.), historical atlas (48p.), and U.S. history atlas (64p.). Very legible.

C660 Cosmopolitan world atlas. Census ed. Chicago: Rand McNally, 1981. Various paging.

About 300 maps, primarily political, with emphasis on the United States and Canada (separate map of each state and province). Index with 82,000 entries.

C661 The great geographical atlas. Chicago: Rand McNally in association with Istituto Geografico de Agostini, Novara, Italy, and Mitchell Beazley Publishers, London, 1982. 304p. Index.

Maps are by the Istituto Geografico de Agostini, supplemented by Rand McNally maps for North America. A 112-page encyclopedia section, prepared by Mitchell Beazley, discusses and illustrates astronomy, earth science, life sciences, environmental science, and cartography. The international map index contains more than 75,000 names; a separate index for Canada and the United States contains 24,000 names.

C662 Kartographisches Institut. Bertelsmann Atlas international. Ed. by W. Bormann. Text in English, French, and German. Gütersloh, W. Germany: C. Bertelsmann, 1975. Various pagings. (1st ed. 1963) (Amer. ed. McGraw-Hill international atlas. New York: McGraw-Hill, 1964. 544p.)

Regional physical maps. Special detailed section for Central Europe. Map scales comparable in various sections. Two separate indexes: world series of plates and Central European section. Total of about 175,000 names.

C663 Pergamon world atlas. Oxford and New York: Pergamon, 1968. 525p. Prepared and printed by the Polish Army Topographical Service (Wojsko Polskie, Shuzba Topograficzna).

Distinguished by large map-surface area, made possible by foldouts. Physical, thematic, and regional maps. Index of 150,000 names.

C664 Atlante internazionale del Touring Club Italiano. 8th ed. Milan: Consociazione Turistica Italiana, 1968. 2v. Maps and index. Updated reprinting 1977.

Detailed reference atlas with large number of place names. Well-designed and well-produced location maps. 93 maps on 173 plates. Relief by hachuring and shading. Index of about 250,000 names.

C665 Russia (1923– USSR). Glavnoe Upravlenie Geodezii i Kartografii (Chief Administration of Geodesy and Cartography). The world atlas. 2d ed. Moscow: 1967. 250 plates. (1st ed. 1954. 283 plates in Russian only)

English-language version of the revised 2d ed. of *Atlas Mira*, with all names in Latin letters and text in English. One of the really fine world atlases. The *Index-gazetteer* (Moscow: 1968, 1,010p.) includes all proper names found on the maps of the atlas, and indicates map location. About 200,000 names. Glossary of geographical terms and key to transliteration system.

Smaller Atlases

C666 Goode's world atlas. 16th ed. Ed. by Edward B. Espenshade, Jr., and Joel L. Morrison. Chicago: Rand McNally, 1982. 368p. (first pub. as Goode's school atlas, 1923. 96, 41p.)

The most widely used, and generally the best, American world atlas for school, home, or office. Convenient and up-to-date small atlas with thematic world maps of physical, cultural, and economic features and regional physical-political maps. Maps of major cities and environs with separate index. Table of world comparisons and data on principal countries and regions of the world. Pronouncing index of 32,000 geographical names, with map locations and latitude and longitude. Recommended for even the smallest library and as a convenient shelf-size atlas to be kept handy for frequent consultation, a source of first resort.

C667 The New York Times atlas of the world: in collaboration with the Times of London. Rev. ed. New York: Times Books, 1981. Various pagings. (1st ed. 1972; rev. ed. 1975, as The Times concise atlas of the world)

Excellent medium-size atlas. Introduction with thematic maps. General reference regional maps. Special maps of metropolitan areas. Index with 90,000 entries.

C668 The new Oxford atlas. Rev. ed. Prepared by the Cartographic Dept. of the Oxford Univ. Pr. London and New York: Oxford Univ. Pr., 1978. 202p. (Oxford atlas, first pub. 1951; New Oxford atlas, 1975)

Regional reference physical-political maps. Maps of oceans, physical environment of the continents. Thematic maps of the world and of the United Kingdom. Gazetteer with about 55,000 entries.

C669 National Geographic Society. Cartographic Div. National Geographic atlas of the world. Rev. 5th ed. Washington, D.C.: The Society, 1981. 383p. (1st ed. 1963. 300p.)

Primarily a location atlas with a large number of place names but also clear depiction of railroads, roads, and various cultural features and physical forms. Index records map location of about 150,000 place-names.

C670 Philip (George) and Son. The university atlas. 17th ed. Ed. by Harold Fullard and H.C. Darby. London: Philip, 1975. 111p. (1st ed. 1937. 96p.)

High-quality small atlas with thematic world maps and regional physical-political maps. Tables of statistical information. Index of 46,000 names indicates map location and latitude and longitude.

Webb, W.H. and associates (1986) *Sources of Information in the Social Sciences, A guide to the literature*, 3rd edition, pp. 204–6 (Chicago: American Library Association).

COMPARING SOURCES, COMPARING IDEAS

Task 13 (Individual)

You are going to study two encyclopaedia entries for a well-known American film actor of the 1940s and 50s. What sort of information do you expect to find? In what order do you expect to find this information? Make a list of headings for note-taking.

Task 14 (Individual)

Study these encyclopaedia entries. What additional information does Text 2 contain compared with Text 1? What information is contained in Text 1 which is not contained in Text 2? Do the entries disagree on any factual detail?

Text 1

BOGART, bō′gärt, **Humphrey** (1899–1957), American stage and screen actor, whose haggard face, sarcastic smile, and gravelly voice made him the archetype of the Hollywood tough guy. He was born in New York City on Jan. 23, 1899, the son of a prosperous surgeon. After attending Trinity School in New York and Phillips Academy in Andover, Mass., he joined the Navy in World War I. Following a brief interlude of professional vagabondage after the war, Bogart made his stage debut in 1920 as a juvenile in a road production of *The Ruined Lady*. For years thereafter he played colorless juveniles.

Bogart's distinctive acting personality was established in 1935, when he played a snarling gangster in *The Petrified Forest*. His recreation of the part for the screen the following year established him in motion pictures. His memorable films include *Casablanca* (1942), *The Maltese Falcon* (1942), *To Have and Have Not* (1945), *Key Largo* (1948), *The Treasure of Sierra Madre* (1948), and *The African Queen* (1951), for which he won an Academy Award.

Bogart was married four times, the last time to the screen actress Lauren Bacall. He died in Hollywood on Jan. 14, 1957.

LOUIS SHEAFFER
Author of "O'Neill, Son and Playwright"

Text 2

Bogart, Humphrey, original name HUMPHREY DEFOREST BOGART (b. Dec. 25, 1899, New York City—d. Jan. 14, 1957, Hollywood), actor who became a preeminent motion picture "tough guy" and was a top box-office attraction during the 1940s and '50s. In his performances he created an image of a weather-beaten, individualistic adventurer with a touch of idealism hidden beneath a deadpan exterior. Offscreen he appeared to be a cynical loner, granting only minimal concessions to Hollywood conventions, and became a cult hero of the American cinema.

The son of a prominent surgeon and a famous illustrator, Bogart served in the United States Navy during World War I. A wood splinter accidentally penetrated his upper lip and stiffened it, giving him a physical characteristic that was later one of his screen trademarks. He began a stage career playing juvenile roles in drawing-room comedies and made his screen debut in *Broadway's Like That* (1930). Achieving little success in films, he returned to New York. His portrayal of the murderer Duke Mantee in the Broadway production of *The Petrified Forest* (1935) and later in the film version (1936) was a turning point in his career. Throughout the late 1930s he was a popular gangster figure in crime pictures starring Edward G. Robinson, James Cagney, and others. In 1941 Bogart attained stardom for his portrayals of Mad Dog Roy Earle, the ageing gangster in *High Sierra* (1941), and then as Sam Spade, the hard-boiled private detective in *The Maltese Falcon* (1941). Other famous characterizations followed, *e.g.*, the expatriate cabaret proprietor Rick in *Casablanca* (1942); the greedy prospector Fred C. Dobbs in *The Treasure of the Sierra Madre* (1948); a gin-drinking boatman in *The African Queen* (1951), for which he won an Academy Award for best actor; the neurotic Captain Queeg in *The Caine Mutiny* (1954); a burnt-out journalist in *The Harder They Fall* (1956). Bogart formed a sensational screen partnership with Lauren Bacall, his fourth wife (whom he married in 1945), in a number of pictures: *To Have and Have Not* (1944), *The Big Sleep* (1946), *Dark Passage* (1947), and *Key Largo* (1948).

Text 1: *Encyclopaedia Americana* (1977) Vol. 4, p. 137 (New York: Americana Corporation).
Text 2: *Encyclopaedia Britannica* (1986) Micropaedia, Vol. 2, p. 323 (Chicago: Encyclopaedia Britannica Inc.).

Task 15 (Individual)

Study this note-taking frame. How does it differ from the list of headings you prepared in Task 13? Complete the frame with information from the sources.

Humphrey Bogart

Dates, birthplace:

_ _

Early life:

_ _

Early acting career:

_ _

Significant films:

_ _

Type of character played:

_ _

Task 16 (Class)

You have all learned English as a second or as a foreign language. The text you are going to read describes a theory of language learning. Before you read, think about these questions:

1. Why do learners make mistakes?
2. What do mistakes tell us?
3. What is the influence of your mother tongue when you learn a foreign language?

The text uses these abbreviations:

L1	First language	FL	Foreign language
L2	Second language	FLL	Foreign language learning

Task 17 (Pairs)

Work in pairs, A and B.

Student A: Your text has these sections:

1. How FLL happens according to behaviourists
2. Influence of L1
3. Aim of behaviourist teaching
4. Problems with the behaviourist view
5. Two problems with imitation
6. Evidence from research
7. Conclusion

Scan Text 1 to mark where each of these sections begins. Then read the text to complete your section of the table on page 130.

Text 1

THE BEHAVIOURIST VIEW

A great deal of language learning and teaching in the 1950s and 1960s was influenced by the tenets of behaviourism (pp. 234, 408). In this view, FLL is seen as a process of imitation and reinforcement: learners attempt to copy what they hear, and by regular practice they establish a set of acceptable habits in the new language. Properties of the L1 are thought to exercise an influence on the course of L2 learning: learners 'transfer' sounds, structures, and usages from one language to the other. A widely used typology distinguishes two kinds of transfer. Similarities between the two languages cause 'positive transfer': it proves acceptable to use the L1 habits in the L2 setting (e.g. the assumption that the subject goes before the verb satisfactorily transfers from English to French). Differences cause 'negative transfer', generally known as 'interference': the L1 habits cause errors in the L2 (e.g. the same assumption about subject–verb order does not satisfactorily transfer into Welsh). Typical interference errors include: *I wait here since 3 hours* (from French) and *How long must my hand in plaster stay?* (from German). Problems of negative transfer are thought to provide a major source of FLL difficulty. The main aim of behaviourist teaching is thus to form new, correct linguistic habits through intensive practice, eliminating interference errors in the process.

There are several problems presented by this account of FLL. Imitation alone does not provide a means of identifying the task facing learners, who are continually confronted with the need to create and recognize novel utterances that go beyond the limitations of the model sentences they may have practised. Nor does imitation suffice as an explanation of the way learners behave: not many of the errors that are theoretically predicted by the differences between L1 and L2 in fact occur in the language of learners; and conversely, other errors are found that seem unrelated to the L1. In a frequently-cited early study (H. C. Dulay & M. K. Burt, 1973), 145 Spanish-speaking children aged 5 to 8 were observed while learning English. Six structures were selected and the error patterns analysed. It emerged that interference errors (such as *They have hunger* from *Ellos tienen hambre*) accounted for only 3% of the errors made. The majority of the errors (85%, with a further 12% unclear) were thought to resemble those that appear in the course of L1 acquisition (e.g. *They hungry*). Analyses of this kind have proved to be controversial (largely because of difficulties in validating the error analysis – see below), but their general conclusion is widely supported. The systematic comparison of L1 and L2, in order to predict areas of greatest learning difficulty – a procedure known as *contrastive analysis* – explains only a small part of what goes on in FLL.

Crystal, D. (1987) *The Cambridge Encyclopedia of Language*, p. 372 (Cambridge: Cambridge University Press).

Student B: Your text has these sections:

1. The cognitive view
2. Definition of interlanguage
3. Role of error analysis
4. Importance of errors
5. Complexity of error analysis
6. Limitations of error analysis
7. Scope of new explanatory models

Scan Text 2 to mark where each of these sections begins. Then read the text to complete your section of the table on page 130.

Text 2

THE COGNITIVE VIEW

The main alternative to the behaviourist approach sees as central the role of cognitive factors in language learning (pp. 234–5). In this view, learners are credited with using their cognitive abilities in a creative way to work out hypotheses about the structure of the FL. They construct rules, try them out, and alter them if they prove to be inadequate. Language learning, in this account, proceeds in a series of transitional stages, as learners acquire more knowledge of the L2. At each stage, they are in control of a language system that is equivalent to neither the L1 nor the L2 – an *interlanguage* (L. Selinker, 1972).

Error analysis plays a central role in this approach. Errors are likely to emerge when learners make the wrong deductions about the nature of the L2, such as assuming that a pattern is general, when in fact there are exceptions. The errors provide positive evidence about the nature of the learning process, as the learner gradually works out what the FL system is. For example, learners who say *vous disez* instead of *vous dites* 'you say' have assumed, wrongly, that the *-ez* ending found after *vous* in most other French verbs (*marchez*, *donnez*, etc.) also applies to *dire* 'say'. The error in this case indicates that a faulty generalization (or analogy, p. 234) has been made.

Since the 1970s, cognitive approaches to FLL have been in the ascendant, and error analysis in particular has attracted a great deal of attention. However, the analysis of errors turns out to be a highly complex matter, involving other factors than the cognitive. Some errors are due to the influence of the mother tongue, as contrastive analysis claims. Some come from external influences, such as inadequate teaching or materials. Some arise out of the need to make oneself understood by whatever means possible (e.g. replacing words by gestures). Moreover, not all errors are equally systematic, disruptive, or unacceptable. Errors of vocabulary, for example, are less general and predictable than errors of grammar, but they are usually more disruptive of communication. Some errors, indeed, become so acceptable that they do not disappear: they become 'fossilized' – tolerated by learners (insofar as they are conscious of them) because they do not cause major problems of communication (e.g. the pronunciation errors that constitute a foreign accent).

Above all, error analysis is complicated by the fact that it is often unclear what the learner intended to say, and thus how to identify the error that has been made. For example, does *The lady eat it* display an error of the noun (*ladies*) or verb – and if the latter, should the correct form be *eats*, *is eating*, *ate*, or some other variant? And even if we assume that the speaker intended to say *eats*, we are still left with the question of whether the error is one of pronunciation (the speaker having difficulty with the [ts] cluster) or grammar – and, within the latter heading, whether the difficulty is one of morphology (lack of awareness of the ending) or syntax (lack of awareness of number agreement between subject and verb) (§16).

Despite the difficulties, research into errors continues to provide a fruitful way of investigating the processes underlying FL acquisition. However, as with contrastive analysis, the approach cannot provide a complete explanation. Most FLL settings do not constitute the kind of 'pure', natural linguistic situation that is presupposed by the cognitive approach, but contains elements of formal teaching, in which learners are systematically introduced to fragments of the L2 (e.g. one tense at a time). To understand the way languages come to be learned in these 'mixed' settings, it is thus proving necessary to devise more sophisticated models,

LIVERPOOL
JOHN MOORES UNIVERSITY
AVRIL ROBARTS LRC
TEL. 0151 231 4022

which focus on the relationship between the processes of natural acquisition and those of formal learning, and which pay adequate attention to the needs and aims of the students, and to the nature of the social setting in which FLL interaction takes place.

Crystal, D. op. cit., p. 373.

Theories of Language Acquisition
Theory – Behaviourist
When influential:
Learning takes place through: 1. 2.
Errors:
Teaching aim:
Problems: 1. 2. 3.
Theory – Cognitive
When influential:
Learning takes place through: 1. 2. 3.
Errors:
Problems: 1. 2. 3.

Task 18 (Pairs)

Exchange notes with your partner to complete both sections of the table.

Unit 11 Using reference sources (2)

One of the problems faced by students and researchers is keeping up-to-date in their field. Journals are a source of up-to-date information, the only problem is having time to read them.

In this unit we will look at how reference sources such as specialist subject indexes and abstracts can help us to find out about the very latest information in our field.

TO MAKE YOU THINK

Task 1 (Individual, then groups)

Make a list of all the journals and periodicals that you are aware of in your field. Add to your list any details such as:

how often they are published
where they are published
who is responsible for their publication
how much they cost

Rate them on a scale of 1–5 according to how often you consult them.

1. Regularly
2. Fairly regularly
3. Occasionally
4. Rarely
5. Never

Compare your results with the rest of your group.

Task 2 (Groups)

Study the list of journals (on pages 132–4) from a specialist index. Which of these disciplines do you feel this index would be most appropriate for?

1. Life Sciences
2. Physical, Chemical and Earth Sciences
3. Social and Behavioural Sciences
4. Agriculture, Biology and Environmental Sciences
5. Clinical Medicine
6. Engineering, Technology and Applied Sciences
7. Arts and Humanities

Task 3 (Individual, then groups)

Tick (√) any titles you recognise. Star (*) any title you feel may be relevant to your field. Compare your list with others in your group.

List of Journals Indexed

Adam International R.
Africa
African Affairs
Agricultural History R.
Ancient Monuments Soc. Trans.
Annals of Science
Antiquaries J.
Antique Collector
Antiquity
Apollo
Archaeologia
Archaeologia Aeliana
Archaeologia Cambrensis
Archaeologia Cantiana
Archaeological J.
Archaeological Reports
Architects' J.
Architectural History
Architectural R.
Archives
Arms Control
Art History
Asian Affairs
Aumla
Australian Historical Studies
Australian Outlook
Author
Banker
Bedfordshire Archaeology
Berkshire Archaeol. J.
Birmingham and Warwickshire Archaeol. Soc. Trans.
Bodleian Library Record
Book Collector
Bookseller
Bristol and Gloucestershire Archaeol. Soc. Trans.
Brit. Academy Proc.
Brit. Archaeol. Assoc. J.
Brit. Book News
Brit. J. for Eighteenth Century Studies
Brit. J. for the History of Science
Brit. J. of Aesthetics
Brit. J. of Criminology
Brit. J. of Industrial Relations
Brit. Library J.
Brit. Numismatic J.
Building
Bull. of Hispanic Studies
Bull. of Latin American Research
Burlington Mag.
Business Archives
Business History
Cambridge Antiquarian Soc. Proc.
Cambridge Bibliographical Soc. Trans.
Cambridge Q.
Ceredigion
Chelys
Chester Archaeol. Soc. J.
Classical Q.
Composer
Connoisseur
Consort
Contemporary Record
Continuity and Change
Costume
Country Life
Criminal Law R.
Critical Q.
Critical R.
Cumberland & Westmorland Antiq. & Archaeol. Soc. Trans.
Derbyshire Archaeol. J.
Devonshire Assoc. Trans.
Dorset Natural History and Archaeol. Soc. Proc.
Drama
Durham Archaeol. J.
Durham University J.
Early Music
Economic Affairs
Economic History R.
Economic R.
Economics
Economist
Encounter
English
English Historical R.
Essays and Studies
Essays in Criticism
Essex Archaeology and History
Financial Times
Folk Music J.
Folklore
French Studies
Furniture History
Galpin Soc. J.
Geographical J.
Geographical Mag.
Geography
German Life and Letters
Government and Opposition
Greece and Rome
Guardian
Hermathena
Historic Soc. of Lancashire and Cheshire Trans.
Historical J.
Historical Research
History
History of European Ideas
History Today
Honourable Soc. of Cymmrodorion Trans.
Howard J.

Illus. London News
Immigrants and Minorities
Independent
Independent on Sunday
Index on Censorship
Industrial Archaeology R.
Inst. of Archaeology Bull.
Intelligence and National Security
International Affairs
International J. of the History of Sport
International Studies Q.
Irish Historical Studies
Italian Studies
John Rylands Library Bull.
J. of African History
J. of American Studies
J. of Common Market Studies
J. of Commonwealth and Comparative Politics
J. of Commonwealth Literature
J. of Communist Studies
J. of Contemporary History
J. of Development Studies
J. of Ecclesiastical History
J. of Garden History
J. of Hellenic Studies
J. of Imperial and Commonwealth History
J. of Industrial Affairs
J. of Industrial Economics
J. of Jewish Studies
J. of Latin American Studies
J. of Law and Society
J. of Legal History
J. of Modern African Studies
J. of Musicological Research
J. of Peasant Studies
J. of Roman Studies
J. of Russian Studies
J. of Southern African Studies
J. of Stained Glass
J. of Strategic Studies
J. of Theological Studies
J. of Transport Economics and Policy
J. of Transport History
Juridical R.
Lancashire and Cheshire Antiq. Soc. Trans.
Landfall
Law Q.R.
Leeds Art Calendar
Leeds Phil. and Literary Soc. Proc.
Leicestershire Historian
Library History
Lincolnshire History and Archaeology
Listener
Literature and Theology
Local Government Studies
Local Historian
Local Population Studies
London and Middlesex Archaeol. Soc. Trans.
London J.
Long Room
Man
Manchester Memoirs
Manx Museum J.
Mariner's Mirror
Medieval Archaeology
Mediterranean Historical R.
Medium Aevum
Middle Eastern Studies
Midland History
Millennium
Mind
Modern Language R.
Modern Law R.
Modern Theology
Montgomeryshire Collections
Month
Monumental Brass Soc. Trans.
Museums J.
Music and Letters
Music R.
Musical Times
National Library of Wales J.
New Humanist
New Left R.
New Scientist
New Statesman and Society
New Zealand J. of History
Norfolk Archaeology
Northamptonshire Past and Present
Northern History
Notes and Queries
Nottingham French Studies
Nottingham Medieval Studies
Observer
Opera
Oral History
Oxford Art J.
Oxford Slavonic Papers
Oxford R. of Economic Policy
Oxoniensia
Parliamentarian
Parliamentary Affairs
Parliamentary History
Past and Present
Personnel Management
Philosophical Q.
Philosophy
Planner
Policy and Politics
Political Q.
Political Science
Political Studies
Prehistoric Soc. Proc.
Printing Historical Soc. J.
Prose Studies
Public Administration
Publishing History
R. of English Studies
R. of International Studies
Race and Class
Radical Philosophy
Radnorshire Soc. Trans.
Ratio
Recusant History
Regional Studies
Religious Studies
Renaissance and Modern Studies
Renaissance Studies

Research Papers: Muslims in Europe
RIBA J.
Royal Asiatic Soc. J.
Royal Historical Soc. Trans.
Royal Musical Assoc. J.
Royal Musical Assoc. Research Chronicle
RSA J.
Scots Mag.
Scottish Archaeol. R.
Scottish Art R.
Scottish Geographical Mag.
Scottish Historical R.
Scottish J. of Political Economy
Scottish J. of Religious Studies
Scottish J. of Theology
Scottish Studies
Service Industries J.
Shropshire Archaeol. Soc. Trans.
Sight and Sound
Slavery and Abolition
Slavonic and East European R.
Sobornost
Soc. for Army Historical Research J.
Soc. for Psychical Research J.
Soc. for Psychical Research Proc.
Soc. of Antiquaries of Scotland Proc.
Soc. of Archivists J.
Social History
Social Studies R.
Somerset Archaeol. and Natural History
Soviet Studies
Spectactor
Staffordshire Studies
Strad
Studio International
Suffolk Inst. of Archaeol. and Hist. Proc.
Sunday Times
Surrey Archaeol. Collections
Sussex Archaeol. Collections
Tempo
Textile History
Theatre Research International
Theology
Third World Planning R.
Third World Q.
Thoroton Soc. Trans.
Times
Times Lit. Suppt.
Town and Country Planning
Town Planning R.
Urban Studies
Warburg and Courtauld Inst. J.
Welsh History R.
West European Politics
Wiltshire Archaeol. and Natural History Mag.
Women's Studies
Women's Studies International Forum
Woolhope Naturalists' Field Club Trans.
Worcestershire Archaeol. Soc. Trans.
World Archaeology
World Development
World Economy
Year's Work in English Studies
Year's Work in Modern Language Studies
Yorkshire Archaeol. J.

British Humanities Index, Vol. 3, 1990, pp. iii–iv.

USING A SPECIALIST INDEX (1)

Task 4 (Individual, then pairs)

What do you understand by these terms?

1. specific headings
2. *see* references
3. related headings
4. *see also* references

Check your answers with this extract (opposite) from the *British Humanities Index* Guide for Users

Using the index

BHI uses specific headings and subheadings, which may be proper names of people or countries or of concepts. 'See' references guide the user from terms not used to those under which entries are to be found. 'Related Heading' references guide the user to other, connected, terms which may be useful. An author index appears at the end of the annual cumulation.

As an example, a user interested in International Relations who starts at the term 'International' will see a list of possible terms there, e.g.

International Law *see* Law, International
International Monetary Fund
International Politics *see* Politics, International
International Trade *see* Trade, International

Some of these, such as **International Monetary Fund**, are followed by the bibliographic details of actual articles. Others direct the user elsewhere in the index, e.g.

International Politics *see* Politics, International

At **Politics, International** are articles on general aspects of international politics, followed by a list of terms, used in that particular issue, where references on related matters may be found:

Politics, International
Related Headings
Colonialism
State Security

Occasionally, there may be a reference which reads *see also* . . . or *see also subhead* . . . These direct the user to a range of possible headings which it would be impracticable to list individually, e.g.

Politics, International *see also subhead* Foreign Affairs under countries

This indicates that the user should look up specific countries of interest, some of which will be found to have entries at the subdivision Foreign Affairs, e.g. **Great Britain: Foreign Affairs**.

Law *see also* Legal . . .

This reminds users who begin their search with the word Law that there may also be terms beginning with the word Legal.

British Humanities Index, op. cit.

Task 5 (Individual, then groups)

Study this example of a reference from the *British Humanities Index*. Identify these items:

1. Journal title
2. Title of article
3. Author
4. Added subtitle
5. Volume
6. Index heading

Changelings
Fairies and the folklore of disability; changelings, hybrids and the solitary fairy. [Relationship between changeling lore and children born with congenital disorders]. Susan Eberly. *Folklore*, 99 (1988) p.58–77. il. ports. refs.

British Humanities Index, op. cit.

Task 6 (Individual)

You are doing research into the teaching and learning of modern languages in the United Kingdom and decide to consult the *British Humanities Index*. Scan this extract from the index and decide which references to follow up.

Lane, Geoffrey, *Baron*
Uneasily astride a fallible system. [Profile]. Simon Lee. *Guardian*, (10 Sep 90) p.17.

Language
Related Headings:
Interpreters
Linguistics
Nonsense
Oaths
Rebuses
Semiotics
Speech
Translations

Language *see also* Individual Languages eg. English Language, French Language, German Language, etc.

Language, Religious
"God-talk" as "tacit" theo-logic. [Use of God-language in non-religious settings]. Shelley Schweizer-Bjelic and Dusan I. Bjelic. *Modern Theology*, 6 (Jul 90) p.341-66. refs.

Languages: Nigeria
Related Headings:
Pidgin English: Nigeria

Languages: Study and Teaching: Great Britain
Modern languages: dead or alive? *Language People: The Experience of Teaching and Learning Modern Languages in British Universities*, by Colin Evans. Christopher Lloyd. *Durham University J.*, 51 (Jul 90) p.255-8. ref.
Speak the lingo in weeks, days — even hours. [Criticism of courses which claim to teach languages rapidly]. Cathy Milton. *Independent*, (16 Aug 90) p.17. refs.

Lapine, James
The song and dance man. [Profile]. Veronica Horwell. *Guardian*, (24 Sep 90) p.34. port.

Larkin, Philip
Into the heart of Englishness. *Philip Larkin: His Life's Work*, by J. Rossen. Tom Paulin. *Times Lit. Suppt.*, (20 Jul 90) p.779-80. ref.
Philip Larkin: the life with a hole in it. [Review article]. John Wiltshire. *Cambridge Q.*, 19 (1990) p.255-65. refs.
Las Palmas
Related Headings:
Art Galleries: Spain: Las Palmas
Lash, Nicholas
Learning to live in holy insecurity: Nicholas Lash's *Easter in Ordinary*. [Interrelation between human experience and knowledge of God]. L. Gregory Jones. *Modern Theology*, 6 (Jul 90) p.385-405. refs.

British Humanities Index, op. cit., p. 127.

USING A SPECIALIST INDEX (2)

Current Contents is a series of specialist indexes. One is published for each of the groups of disciplines listed in Task 2.

1. Life Sciences
2. Physical, Chemical and Earth Sciences
3. Social and Behavioural Sciences
4. Agriculture, Biology and Environmental Sciences
5. Clinical Medicine
6. Engineering, Technology and Applied Sciences
7. Arts and Humanities

Task 7 (Individual)

Study these extracts from the front covers of three versions of *Current Contents*. Decide which versions they are from.

INCLUDING
Biochemistry • Biomedical Research
Biophysics • Chemistry
Cytology/Histology • Endocrinology
Experimental Medicine • Genetics
Hematology • Immunology
Microbiology • Molecular Biology
Neurosciences • Oncology
Pathology • Pharmacology
Pharmaceutics • Physiology
Toxicology

A

INCLUDING
Aesthetics • Archaeology
Architecture • Art • Classics • Dance
Cultural Studies • Film • Folklore
History • History & Philosophy of
Science • Language • Linguistics
Literary Reviews • Literature
Music • Oriental Studies
Philosophy • Poetry • Radio/TV
Religion • Theater

B

INCLUDING
Anthropology • Area Studies
Business • Communication
Economics • Education • Geography
History • Information Science
International Relations • Law
Library Science • Linguistics
Management • Planning &
Development • Political Science
Psychiatry • Psychology
Public Health • Rehabilitation
Social Issues • Social Medicine
Social Work • Sociology
Special Education

C

Task 8 (Individual)

KALEVA

	CC Pg	J Pg
KALEVALA	29	364
KALISPEL	32	87
KALLGREN,JK	106	413
KAMPHOEFNER, WD	32	127
KANE,RA	75	1164
KANIGEL,R	84	376
KANTER,RM	123	75
KANTIAN	45	495
KAPFERER,B	30	491
KAPLAN,JJ	113	767
KARADY,V	113	763
KARASCH,MC	100	460
KARDOS,L	51	229
KARLSEN,CF	100	433
KARNATAKA	99	2359
KASER,DAVID	85	573
KASHMIR	100	57
KASL,SV	58	273
KATZ,B	85	568
KATZ,N	106	408
KATZENSTEIN,PJ	97	606
KAUFMAN,T	35	513
KAWINGA	108	413
KEANE,MT	50	581
KEEPER	56	491
KEI-ISLANDS	29	193
KEIZER,P	115	386
KELLOGG,S	100	449
KELLY,A	46	111
KELLY,J	35	539
KELLYBYRNE,D	38	348
KEMP,BJ	28	686
KEMPF,H	97	598
KENDALL,P	68	794
KENNEDY,D	77	507
KENYA	27	442
	"	451
	110	37
KEPT	88	10
KERNAGHAN,K	97	579
KERSHAW,B	74	1348
KETO,CT	27	445
KEVEKORDES,B	46	134
KEYMATH	84	311
KEYNES	115	342
	119	179
KEYNESIAN	113	754
KEYSER,DJ	80	185
KEYSERLINGK, RH	100	547
KEYWORDS	96	298

KHAL,G

	CC Pg	J Pg
KHAL,GEORGES	97	573
KHALIDI,O	106	406
KHANTHACHAI,N	106	423
KIMBALL,R	85	571
KIMMERLING,B	107	127
KIMURA,Y	32	142
KIND	48	492
KINDERGARTEN	84	325
KINGDOM	32	99
	96	259
KINSHIP	38	149
	"	170
	"	198
	"	215
	"	241
	100	471
KIPLE,KF	31	106
KITAB	29	226
KITZINGER,S	79	392
KIVISTO,P	32	119
KKRISTIANSEN,K	94	896
KLEIN,M	51	223
	"	224
KLEIN,SB	65	433
	"	435
KLEJMAN,L	97	629
KLEPTOMANIA	68	770
KLINE,J	41	142
KLOOS,H	39	527
KLOSE,DAO	28	704
KNEE	52	435
KNOSSOS	28	689
KNOT	70	669
KNOW-HOW	112	645
KNOWING	48	571
	51	221
KNOWLEDGE	28	702
	48	571
	56	377
	58	412
	65	777
	71	1046
	77	425
	"	496
	"	504
	93	763
	97	632
	113	773
	120	257
	124	531
KNOWLEDGE-BASED	90	327
KNOWS	116	51
KODAMA,K	108	468
KOENKER,DP	109	827
KOFAS,JV	100	549
KOGAN,M	47	581
KOHL,HELMUT	110	234
	"	236
KOMLOS,J	38	370
KONIG,C	27	451
KONINKLIJK	29	376
KOPPERMAN,PE	100	490
KOREAN	32	144

KOREAN

	CC Pg	J Pg
KOREAN (cont)	70	703
	100	454
KORNBLUH,H	122	585
KOROTH	94	888
KRAFONA,K	27	435
KRAGH,H	46	123
KRIEGER,G	83	309
KRIO	27	450
	37	845
KRIVANEK,J	63	287
KRIYOL	37	713
KRONOS	71	1036
KROUT,JA	49	131
KRUPINSKI,J	51	220
KRUYT,B	43	235
KTH	43	271
	"	375
KUHLENBECK,H	31	97
KUHN	83	34
KUHN,HJ	31	94
KUHN,JH	46	124
KUIPERS,SK	115	350
KUMMER,B	31	94
KUNING	29	226
KUPER,GH	115	350
KUROMIYA,H	100	529
KUSHNER,T	100	535
KWAZULU	121	88
LABELS	64	383
LABOR	29	349
	38	273
	43	231
	89	362
	100	450
	"	451
	"	524
	"	534
	"	539
	"	550
	106	400
	109	701
	115	384
	120	31
	122	591
	123	32
	124	481
	"	585
	"	616
	"	625
	"	635
LABOR-MARKET	109	701
	124	643
LABORATORY-ANIMAL	63	215
LACK	75	1127
LACORNE,D	97	598
LACTATING	65	401
LACUNA	68	781
LAFLAMME,G	124	643
LAGOONS	96	209
LAGS	65	693
LAMARCK	46	163
LAMB,A	99	2425

LAMBER

	CC Pg	J Pg
LAMBERGKAR-LOVSKY,CC	28	679
LAMOUREUX,D	97	585
LAMP	43	155
LAMSON,A	51	227
LAND	27	448
	"	451
	32	80
	43	242
	99	2385
	100	522
	106	400
LAND-EN	29	376
LAND-USE	43	232
	92	279
	115	367
LANDED	100	519
LANDFILL	91	269
LANDSCAPE	28	710
	87	387
	92	337
LANE,JB	32	139
LANGEP-FAUTSCH,R	46	144
LANGER,FELICIA	107	24
LANGERHANS	46	147
LANGFORD,JW	97	579
LANGFORD,P	100	499
LANGSTON, JOHN,MERCER	100	448
LANGUAGE	31	105
	34	511
	"	625
	"	719
	"	728
	35	363
	"	513
	"	518
	36	1
	"	5
	"	37
	"	101
	"	119
	"	153
	"	175
	37	661
	"	883
	50	569
	59	941
	60	697
	65	850
	81	103
	84	296
	97	531
	"	537
LANGUAGE, NAT-URAL	35	543
	87	3
LANGUAGE-ERROR	30	285
LANGUAGE-LEARNING	40	443
	"	445
	50	574
LAPTOP	86	328
LARONDE,A	28	698
LAROSA,V	28	699
LARSEN,M	94	896
LASERDISC	88	37
LASLETT,P	38	363
LATE-18TH	39	519
LATENT	40	427
	62	442
LATERAL	50	519
LATERALITY	61	1011
LATERALIZATION	26	113
	"	357

LATERA

	CC Pg	J Pg
LATERALIZATION (cont)	67	241
LATIN	32	139
LATIN-AMERICA	43	174
	44	520
LATIN-AMERICAN	44	520
LATINA	44	519
LATOUCHE,D	97	586
LAURENT,G	46	163
LAW	25	A 101
	32	87
	45	651
	"	676
	47	587
	64	383
	94	839
	97	590
	"	621
	100	456
	"	516
	112	620
	"	1338
	"	1358
	115	375
	116	28
	"	32
	124	585
	"	625
	"	637
	"	640
LAWRENCE,BS	118	456
LAWTON,R	39	519
	113	765
LAYBOURN,K	100	524
	"	534
	113	752
LAYBOURNE,K	100	534
LAYMANS	36	57
LAZERSON,A	31	96
LDCS	120	73
LDI	84	339
LE-CONTE-POURQUOI	29	364
LEAD	108	469
LEADER	29	337
	"	349
	32	126
	36	36
	45	515
	56	500
	67	139
	82	89
	100	539
LEADERSHIP	25	A 1
	"	B 41
	"	B 163
	36	99
	60	641
	74	1326
	86	403
	88	306
	97	568
	123	44
	"	77
LEAF	32	135
LEARN	81	108
	123	75
LEARNED	81	369
LEARNERS	81	109
LEARNING	36	55
	44	463
	49	21
	50	377
	53	213
	"	1241
	58	412
	61	415
	"	1035
	65	385
	"	433
	"	435
	"	777
	70	728
	74	1348
	79	249
	"	304
	"	356
	80	181

LEARNI

	CC Pg	J Pg
LEARNING (cont)	81	90
	"	108
	83	251
	"	311
	117	980
	122	585
LEARNING DISABILITIES	84	339
LEARNING DISABLED	84	289
LEAST-SQUARES	40	387
	"	405
LEAVE	47	401
LEAVING	47	535
	"	592
	68	797
LEBANESE	106	723
LEBANON	49	47
LEBEDINSKAJA, GV	31	102
LEBOHEC,Y	94	891
LEBOULLUEC,A	94	871
LECTURE	35	513
	56	443
LEE,H	39	519
	113	765
LEEUWARDEN	36	1
	"	175
LEGACY	71	1051
	100	438
	115	256
LEGAL	26	195
	99	2351
	112	1393
	115	377
	124	531
LEGENDRE,P	97	594
LEGENDS	30	491
LEGISLATION	42	585
	92	347
	97	577
LEGISLATIVE	25	A 139
LEGITIMATE	42	613
LEGITIMATING	36	77
LEGOFF,J	100	417
LEHISTE,I	35	513
LEIBENSTEIN, HARVEY	118	462
LEILAN	28	684
LEISURE	41	309
	"	337
	77	417
LEITMOTIF	31	72
LENDING	120	388
LENDS	124	647
LENEMAN,L	100	522
LENGTH-OF-STAY	42	621
LENNERSTRAND, G	30	377
LEOBERSDORF	31	102
LEON	118	307
LEONARD,BE	68	796
LEONE	27	450
LEPAGE,L	97	562

LESAGE

	CC Pg	J Pg
LESAGE,M	97	564
LESBIAN	29	344
LESION	61	1011
	"	1021
LESLAU,W	37	351
LESSON	47	579
	75	1151
	81	92
	"	407
	121	21
LETHARGIC	68	770
LETTER BY LETTER	61	1079
LETTERS	32	127
	97	586
	100	447
	"	511
	"	527
LEVELT,WJM	65	853
LEVIATHAN	46	134
LEVINE,D	100	453
LEVITAN,M	31	92
LEVY,B	100	434
LEVY,DC	36	103
LEWIS,J	93	753
LEWIS,OJ	31	94
LEWIS,PG	109	825
LEXICAL	34	677
LEXIS	85	15
LEY,ROBERT	100	539
LEYMANN,H	122	585
LIBERAL	115	340
LIBERAL-ARTS-COLLEGE-LIBRARY	85	524
LIBERALISM	30	431
	34	190
	97	419
	"	598
LIBERALIZATION	106	359
LIBERATION	107	122
LIBERTY	100	435
	"	466
LIBRARIAN	87	411
	88	98
	"	302
	"	306
	89	320
	"	384
	"	387
LIBRARIANSHIP	85	573
	89	376
	"	380
LIBRARY	85	81
	"	105
	"	513
	"	539
	"	553
	"	564
	"	568
	86	326
	"	344
	"	391
	"	403
	87	421
	88	6
	"	98
	"	276
	"	285
	"	291
	"	305
	"	307
	89	366
	"	370
	"	374
	"	375
	"	377
	"	381
	"	382
	"	383

LIBRAR

	CC Pg	J Pg
LIBRARY (cont)	90	355
LIBRARY, PUBLIC	88	98
LIBYA	28	698
LICENSING	112	645
LICHTSINN,H	31	100
LIDEN,K	30	511
LIEBERSON,S	32	115
	39	521
LIFE	31	105
	"	106
	32	94
	38	348
	"	363
	41	367
	42	803
	44	521
	"	527
	46	134
	"	139
	"	151
	"	152
	47	368
	55	393
	56	572
	59	1040
	64	362
	75	1164
	100	431
	"	449
	"	460
	"	473
	"	480
	"	493
	"	494
	113	774
LIFE, EARLY	35	163
LIFE-CYCLE	38	301
	41	395
	60	657
	120	446
LIFE-SPAN	66	419
	67	318
LIFESTYLES	39	522
LIFETIME	81	92
LIGHT	53	1201
	63	240
	80	461
	99	2405
	118	889
LIGHT,LL	50	569
LIKABILITY	60	641
LILLEY,DB	89	361
LIMES	94	899
LIMIT	47	575
	53	1231
	100	436
LIMITATIONS	42	785
	68	645
	71	1060
	89	372
	97	627
LIMITED	60	693
	82	269
LIMQUECO,P	106	399
LINCOLN	100	442
LINDBECK,A	122	582
LINDERT,PH	113	59
LINDHOLT,PJ	100	431
LINE	61	1043
LINEAR	40	345
	93	719
LINGUISTIC	31	1
	35	513
	37	370
	"	641
	43	293
	67	281
LINK	48	516
	52	413

Current Contents: Social and Behavioural Sciences, Vol. 22, No. 51, 17 Dec. 1990.

Current Contents contains a Title Word Index. This is a computer-produced alphabetical listing of the significant words in every article and book title listed in each issue. At the top of each column, the abbreviations CC Pg and J Pg appear. These refer to *Current Contents* page and Journal page.

Scan the index page on page 138 for the entry 'Language Learning'. Note the *Current Contents* page and Journal page for each entry.

Task 9 (Individual)

Here are the appropriate pages from *Current Contents*. Locate the articles and write down the references in full.

CONTINUED POP STUD-J DEMOGR,44(3)90

Infant Mortality in India - Differentials and Determinants, by A.K. Jain, P. Visaria. *P.N.M. Bhat* 515

Growing Old in the 20th-Century, by M. Jefferys. *P. Laslett* 517

Pregnancy, Contraception and Family Planning Services in Industrialized Countries, by E.F. Jones, J.D. Forrest, S.K. Henshaw, J. Silverman, A. Torres. *A. Leathard* 518

Urban Population Development in Western Europe from the Late-18th to the Early-20th-Century, by R. Lawton, R. Lee. *P.J. Atkins* 519

From Many Strands - Ethnic and Racial Groups in Contemporary America, by S. Lieberson, M.C. Waters. *J. Jupp* 521

Lifestyles, Contraception and Parenthood, by H. Moors, J. Schoorl. *M.N. Bhrolchain* 522

Determinants of Population Growth in India, by G. Ramachandrudu. *V.S. Raleigh* 523

Perspectives on Development and Population Growth in the Third-World, by O.G. Simmons. *A.G. Hill* 524

Population and Resources in Western Intellectual Traditions, by M.S. Teitelbaum, J.M. Winter. *P. Kreager* 525

Ageing in Developing Countries, by K. Tout. *G.W. Jones* 526

The Ecology of Health and Disease in Ethiopia, by Z.A. Zein, H. Kloos. *A. Dewaal* 527

EH754 — **QUALITY & QUANTITY** — KLUWER ACADEMIC PUBL

ARTICLES AND ABSTRACTS IN ENGLISH

VOL.24 NO.4 NOVEMBER 1990

SPECIAL ISSUE: STRUCTURAL EQUATION MODELLING - INTERNATIONAL CONFERENCE ON SOCIAL SCIENCE METHODOLOGY

Special Issue of the Journal Quality and Quantity - Preface. *W.E. Saris* 343

Identification Structure of Linear Structural Models. *G. Seidel, C. Eicheler* 345

Robustness Issues in Structural Equation Modeling - A Review of Recent Developments. *A. Satorra* 367

New Developments in LISREL - Analysis of Ordinal Variables Using Polychoric Correlations and Weighted Least Squares. *K.G. Joreskog* 387

A Panel Model for Political Efficacy and Responsiveness - An Application of LISREL-7 with Weighted Least Squares. *A.M. Aish, K.G. Joreskog* 405

Latent State-Trait Models in Attitude Research. *R. Steyer, M.J. Schmitt* 427

Searching for Parsimony - Are True-Score Models or Factor Models More Appropriate. *W. Jagodzinski, S.M. Kuhnel, P. Schmidt* 447

Common Factors Can Always Be Found But Can They Also Be Rejected. *W.E. Saris, H. Hartman* 471

EJ438 — **SIMULATION & GAMING** — SAGE PUBL INC (USA)

ARTICLES AND ABSTRACTS IN ENGLISH

VOL.21 NO.4 DECEMBER 1990

A Q-Study of Game Player Aesthetics. *D. Myers* 375

In-Basket Exercises As a Methodology for Studying Information Processing. *J.M. Dukerich, F.J. Milliken, D.A. Cowan* 397

The Impact of Goal Setting on Team Simulation Experience. *P.M. Fandt, W.D. Richardson, H.M. Conner* 411
Demand Equations for Business Simulations with Market Segments. *R.D. Teach* 423

COMPUTERIZED SIMULATIONS AND GAMES FOR LANGUAGE LEARNING: PART I

Guest Editorial. *D.W. Coleman* 443
Language Learning Through Computer Adventure Games. *A. Baltra* 445
The Immigrants - The Irish Experience in Boston 1840-1859. *P.A. Mulligan, K. Gore* 453

CONTINUED

40 © 1990 by ISI® CURRENT CONTENTS®

PSYCHOLOGY

EH871 **ACTA PSYCHOLOGICA**
ARTICLES AND ABSTRACTS IN ENGLISH
ELSEVIER SCI PUBL BV, PHYS SCI ENG DIV

VOL.75 NO.1 OCTOBER 1990

Inattention to P(H) and to P(D/Approximately H) - A Converging Operation. *M.E. Doherty, C.R. Mynatt* 1
A Stochastic Model for Inter-Keypress Times in a Typing Task. *R.A. Heath, C.H. Willcox* 13
Auditory Accessory Effects on Visual Processing. *P.J.G. Keuss, F. Vanderzee, M.B.M. Vandenbree* 41
Interference with Visual Short-Term Memory. *R.H. Logie, G.M. Zucco, A.D. Baddeley* 55
Eye Movement Indices of Mental Workload. *J.G. May, R.S. Kennedy, M.C. Williams, W.P. Dunlap, J.R. Brannan* 75

BOOK REVIEWS

Theories of Visual Perception, by I.E. Gordon. *P.G. Vos* 91
The Nature of Creativity - Contemporary Psychological Perspectives, by R.J. Sternberg. *J.J. Elshout* 92
Human Skills, 2nd Edition, by D.H. Holding. *H. Heuer* 95
Cognition and Action in Skilled Behaviour, by A.M. Colley, J.R. Beech. *T. Mulder* 98
Acquisition and Performance of Cognitive Skills, by A.M. Colley, J.R. Beech. *T. Mulder* 98

EH577 **AMERICAN JOURNAL OF PSYCHOLOGY**
ARTICLES AND ABSTRACTS IN ENGLISH
UNIV ILLINOIS PRESS

VOL.103 NO.4 WINTER 1990

William James, The Principles of Psychology, and Experimental Psychology. *R.B. Evans* 433
Utility Functions for Nonmonetary Events. *E. Galanter* 449
Interaction of Attentional and Motor Control Processes in Handwriting. *T.L. Brown, E.E. Donnenwirth* 471
Time Errors in the Method of Pair Comparisons. *S.C. Masin, A. Agostini* 487
Psychology of Novice and Expert Wine Talk. *G.E.A. Solomon* 495
Letter Identification and Lateral Masking in Dyslexic and Average Readers. *P. Goolkasian, J. King* 519

BOOK REVIEWS

The Principles of Psychology, by W. James. *D.W. Massaro* 539
——. *G.S. Hall* 546
The Making of Cognitive Science - Essays in Honor of George A. Miller, by W. Hirst. *I. Pollack* 560
Memory and Amnesia - An Introduction, by A.J. Parkin. *M.S. Weldon* 565
Language, Memory, and Aging, by L.L. Light, D.M. Burke. *L.A. Thompson* 569
Advances in Applied Psycholinguistics, Vol 2, Reading, Writing, and Language Learning, by S. Rosenberg. *J.S. Huitema, K. Rayner* 574
Analogical Problem Solving, by M.T. Keane. *D.R. Smith* 581

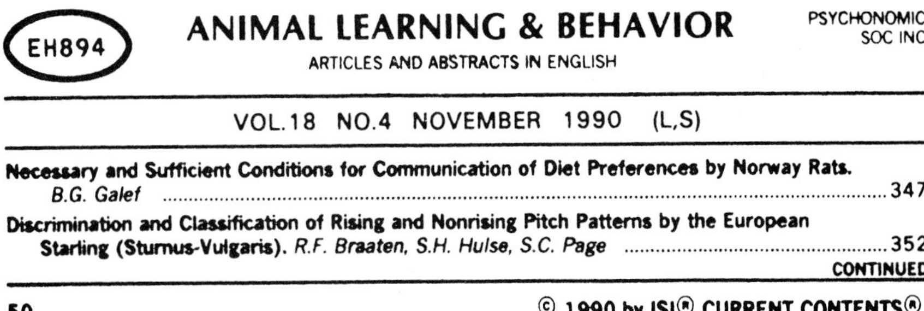

EH894

ANIMAL LEARNING & BEHAVIOR

ARTICLES AND ABSTRACTS IN ENGLISH

PSYCHONOMIC SOC INC

VOL.18 NO.4 NOVEMBER 1990 (L,S)

Necessary and Sufficient Conditions for Communication of Diet Preferences by Norway Rats. *B.G. Galef* 347

Discrimination and Classification of Rising and Nonrising Pitch Patterns by the European Starling (Sturnus-Vulgaris). *R.F. Braaten, S.H. Hulse, S.C. Page* 352

CONTINUED

50 **© 1990 by ISI® CURRENT CONTENTS®**

USING ABSTRACTS

An abstract is a summary of a journal article. Abstract collections are useful to the researcher because they provide both a brief summary of the articles in one's field and a reference so that the original article can be traced.

Task 10 (Individual, then class)

List the titles of any abstract collections you are familiar with. Note any extra information such as publishing details and frequency of publication. Share the information with the class.

Task 11 (Individual)

Study this introduction to a specialist abstract collection. Scan the introduction to find:

1. How often the journal is published
2. Where it is published
3. The aims
4. The coverage
5. The countries represented on the editorial board

Sociology of Education Abstracts

EDITOR
Professor Roger Dale, *Department of Education, University of Auckland*

ASSISTANT EDITOR
Graham Hobbs, *Carfax Information Systems*

EDITORIAL BOARD
Professor W. A. L. Blyth, *School of Education, University of Liverpool*
Professor Louis Cohen, *Department of Education, Loughborough University of Technology*
Professor Maurice Craft, *Hong Kong University of Science and Technology*

LIVERPOOL
JOHN MOORES UNIVERSITY
AVRIL ROBARTS LRC
TEL. 0151 231 4022

Professor E. Stones, *School of Education, University of Liverpool*
Professor D. F. Swift, *Open Learning Institute, Hong Kong*
Professor L. E. Watson, *Centre for Education Management & Administration, Sheffield City Polytechnic*

Sociology of Education Abstracts, first published in 1965, draws on a wide range of international sources as a means of serving the information needs of those concerned with the sociological study of education. The service provides coverage of some 600 journal articles and books each year, in four quarterly issues. Abstracts are prepared by an international team of subject specialists, are non-evaluative in form, and are accompanied by detailed bibliographical citations. Coverage of the service is broad to incorporate the diverse types of material that are relevant to study in this area. Journals from throughout the world and a comprehensive list of publishers' catalogues are scanned regularly for appropriate items. The service can be used both as a means of keeping up to date with newly published material, aided by the provision of author and subject indexes in each issue, and for the purpose of retrospective retrieval, facilitated by annually cumulated author and subject indexes bound in the final issue of each volume.

Editorial and business correspondence, including orders and remittances relating to subscriptions and back numbers, should be addressed to the publishers: Carfax Publishing Company, P.O. Box 25, Abingdon, Oxfordshire OX14 3UE, United Kingdom.

The journal is published quarterly, in March, June, September and December. These four issues constitute one volume.

ISSN 0038-0415

Sociology of Education Abstracts, Vol. 26, No. 2, Journals Oxford Ltd, 1990.

Task 12 (Individual)

Study this sample entry.

2

1

3

82S/464 **A study of pupils suspended from schools.** D. GALLOWAY, *British Journal of Educational Psychology*, 52(2), 1982, pp 205–212. 4

5

This paper reports the results of a study of pupils who had been suspended from school for disciplinary reasons. The results suggest that the pupils were disturbed
6 constitutionally, and presented severe educational problems which were independent of their behaviour. It is argued that these pupils would cause concern at any school, but that variables within their schools were critical in determining whether their behaviour resulted in suspension.

Match each number (1–6) with the correct heading from this list.

a) Abstract
b) Article title
c) Article details
d) Author(s) or Editor(s)
e) Journal title
f) Abstract number

Task 13 (Individual)

You are still interested in the subject of *Teaching and Learning Foreign Languages*. Articles are indexed under 'significant terms' – key words taken from the article title or from the abstract. Scan this extract from the cumulative subject index to find likely significant terms. Note the reference numbers of possible articles.

knowledge, 081

labour market, 094, 378, 508, 531
laissez-faire, 169
language-minority students, 456
language policies, 334
languages, 038, 205, 417
Latinos, 456
learning, 478
leaving examinations, 039
leftist ethnography, 073
legislation, 194
lesbians, 493
liberal arts, 306
liberal justice, 269
literacy, 210, 290, 305
literacy learning, 198
literary theory, 446
local education authorities, 092
logic of accumulation, 221
London, 492

Malawi, 096
male/female dualism, 209
Maltese, 434
management, 092, 117, 123, 131, 432, 491
management of change, 206
management training, 080
managerial ethics, 108
Manpower Services Commission, 015

Task 14 (Individual)

Study these four references which are cited in the index. Match them to the abstracts given below.

1 **Te Reo O Te Tai Tokerau: language, evaluation and empowerment.** M. PETERS and J. MARSHALL, *New Zealand Journal of Educational Studies*, 24 (2), 1989, pp 141–157.

2 **The language of German philosophies of education between World War 1 and 2: holism criticized.** (in Dutch) J.D. IMELMAN, *Comenius*, 36, 1989, pp 501–516.

3 **The controversy over teaching medium in Hong Kong – an analysis of a language policy.** M.S. YAU, *Journal of Multilingual and Multicultural Development*, 10 (4), 1989, pp 279–295.

4 **Languages and political purpose: the Canadian case.** D. RAY, *Canadian and International Education*, 19 (1), 1990, pp 4–15.

Sociology of Education Abstracts, op. cit., pp. 221, 164, 94, 15.

A In Canada there are four justifications for teaching languages. First is Aboriginal status, a claim that is available to a small population, and has seldom been used effectively. The second is official status, accessible to the substantial English and French communities and exercised with varying success. The third is heritage language, which in Canada requires that the language was spoken by ancestors of the claimant and that enough persons are willing to support the claim. The fourth argument is that of utility—that Canadians find political, economic or cultural reasons to learn another language. The first two arguments may be termed rights in the Canadian situation and the latter two are essentially political concessions or privileges backed by common sense.

B This paper analyses a language plan proposed by the Hong Kong government to promote Chinese medium education. A brief history of the past language situation in the secondary school system is first provided followed by an outline of the evolution of the proposed plan. Then the targets set up in the plan are examined against the background of the existing language requirements in the field of education and employment. Since the English-biased linguistic infrastructure in the wider social setting does not correlate to the targets to be promoted in school, it is predicted that the proposed plan will not achieve much success. Moreover, the failure of the plan may even lead to the perpetuation of the inferiority of Chinese medium education.

C This paper describes the project Te Reo O Te Tai Tokerau and its community-oriented, empowerment-styled evaluation. The first section provides a context for a description of the project and its evaluation by briefly summarising some of the issues facing Maori as a School Certificate Examination subject. It also details the development work carried out by the Department of Education since 1984 which prepared the ground for the initiation of Teo Reo O Te Tai Tokerau. The second section describes the evaluation and the model on which it was based, and presents the findings of the evaluation. Finally, the third section indicates subsequent policy and research directions that have emerged since the project was completed.

D The 'geisteswissenschaftliche pädagogik' was during the first half of the 20th century the most important philosophy of education on the European continent. Some other theories, e.g. the proto-nazistic philosophy of Ernst Krieck and the school theory of Peter Petersen (the so-called Jena-Plan) are akin to this philosophy. At this very moment many 'new schools' in Germany and The Netherlands are based on Petersen's ideas. In the meantime one can criticise some aspects of this plan insofar as they are related to essential ways of thinking within the 'geisteswissenschaftliche' tradition. In this article four inter-related positions are defended: (1) the 'geisteswissenschaftliche' philosophy of education is a specimen of system-theoretical thinking (like Schleimacher's Ethik); (2) the concept of 'pedagogical autonomy' refers to education as a subsystem within the overall system of man-in-society-and-culture; (3) in spite of critical pretensions the discourse is suffering from vague, ambiguous and 'holistic' terms. Therefore any historical situation can be judged as 'good'. Perhaps that is one of the reasons why Flitner, Nohl, Petersen, Spranger and others did not recognise the evil of the Third Reich; and (4) their call for reflection is not consistent with and cannot be justified in terms of their philosophy. —*English summary*

Sociology of Education Abstracts, op. cit., p. 289.

Key

Unit 1 Getting to know your textbook

Task 1

1. k
2. d
3. f
4. i
5. h
6. c
7. a
8. b
9. j
10. e
11. g

appendix: Additional information, often for reference purposes, found at the end of a book
bibliography: 1. Sources used to prepare a book or article, usually found at the end; 2. A list of books, articles, etc., arranged by theme
foreword: A short introduction to a book written not by the author but by someone familiar with the author's work

Task 2

A index
B contents
C glossary
D introduction/preface
E publishing details
F title page
G back cover (or dust jacket blurb)

Task 4

1. dust jacket: lines 3–4
2. title page: lines 6–8
3. publishing details: lines 8–11
4. foreword/preface/introduction: lines 13–15
5. table of contents: lines 15–20
6. index: lines 24–6
7. bibliography: lines 27–8

Task 5

1. front cover or title page
2. front cover or title page
3. publishing details
4. publishing details (absence of information means first edition)
5. preface/introduction or back cover
6. preface/introduction, sometimes back cover
7. contents or preface/introduction, sometimes back cover
8. preface/introduction, sometimes contents or back cover

Task 7

1. 233 (108 is an illustration)
2. 433
3. *not given*
4. 259–72 (the other references may be minor)
5. 163 or 166 (both are illustrations)
6. 139–44 (the other references may be minor)
7. 32
8. 156–62 (the other references may be minor)
9. 385
10. any of the pages given, 109, 110, 160, 274, 435, 437

Task 8

1. e
2. j
3. g
4. i
5. h
6. c
7. b
8. a
9. d
10. f

Task 9

Line 2 'This book' (line 1)
Line 4 those people/students
Line 5 engineering
Line 8 careers, education and training (line 6)

Line 10 'This book' (line 8)
Line 12 of textbooks (line 11)
Line 13 Making specific recommendations of textbooks (line 12)
Line 16 the like of reference books
Line 17 details of selected books (line 15)
Line 18 general information provided in certain chapters (line 14)

Task 10

1. Chapter 4
2. Chapter 1
3. Chapter 5
4. Chapter 2
5. Chapter 6
6. Chapter 7

Unit 2 Choosing what to read

Task 1

1. Brown, M.
2. Phillips, E.M. & Pugh, D.S.
3. Maddox, H. *or* Rowntree, D.
4. Dunleavy, P.
5. Borg, W.R. & Gall, M.D.
6. Higbee, K.L.
7. Rowntree, D. *or* Maddox, H.

Task 2

1. 6 Concentration and speed
2. 3 The assessment system
3. 10 Putting anxiety in its place
4. 7 Learning in lectures *or*
   8 Three ways of writing notes
5. 4 Organising your time
6. 10 Preparing for examinations
7. 9 Analysing your task
8. 1 The secrets of success?

Task 3

1. lines 18–19
2. lines 30–3

About 85% of the text can be ignored.

Task 4

1. XXII, possibly XXIII
2. XV
3. XIX
4. XXIV
5. XXVII
6. XIII
7. XXIII
8. XVIII
9. X

Task 6

Group A (Examples)
1. How can we best prepare for examinations?
2. How can we avoid being over-anxious about examinations?
3. What examination techniques are there?
4. How can we best organise subject knowledge for an examination?
5. How can we become skilled in examination techniques?

Group B (Examples)
1. How can we best prepare for examinations?
2. How should we review for examinations?
3. How can we schedule revision?
4. How can we avoid anxiety?
5. What examination techniques are there?

Task 10

1. Difficulty in organising and timetabling work (line 6)
2. Their course may be less structured than previously experienced (lines 12–13)

Task 12

Some suggestions from students on how to find the exact meaning of a word:
1. Use an English–English dictionary.
2. Use an English–my language dictionary.
3. Ask a fellow student.
4. If the word is a specialist term, check the glossary of the textbook.
5. Check the index in case the word is defined in the text when it is first mentioned.

Task 13

a) noun *television, telephone*
b) verb *have*
c) past participle *tempted*
d) adjective *successful*
e) adjective *domestic*
f) noun *ventilation*
g) adverb *likely*
h) verb *should*
i) adjective *filing*
j) noun *timetable*
k) preposition *about*
l) adjective *special*
m) verb *disturb*

Task 14

1. What is memory?
2. What do we mean by 'a good memory'?
3. What are the stages of memory?
4. What is the difference between short-term and long-term memory?
5. How do we measure memory?
6. In what form do we best remember material?
7. Why do we forget?

Task 15 (Examples)

1. What is the difference between short-term and long-term memory?
2. Why do we forget things?
3. How can we retain information in short-term memory?

Paragraph 3 refers.

Unit 3 The spirit of enquiry

Task 2

Words to ignore are *passerine*, *pied flycatcher*, and Latin terms. *Ornithologist* can be worked out from the context. *Nesting-box traps* (line 8) should help refine ideas for a suitable experiment.

Task 4

In addition to the order in the text, one possible order would be:
hypothesis, *predict*, *investigation*, *results*, *significant*, *confirmed*, *suggest*, *conclude*

Task 5

1. b	7. b
2. a	8. b
3. a	9. a
4. b	10. a
5. a	11. a
6. b	12. b

Task 6

Why male birds sing

Most ornithologists take it for granted that male passerine (perching) birds sing to attract females. But, until now, no one has produced any direct evidence to support the idea. Although the males of many species certainly sing much less once they have acquired their mates, and some female birds respond to male song with courtship display, this evidence is circumstantial. Now Dag Eriksson and Lars Wallin, two zoologists from the University of Uppsala in Sweden, have proved the point – for two species at least (*Behavioural Ecology and Sociobiology*, vol. 19, p. 297).

Eriksson and Wallin studied the pied flycatcher (Ficedula hypoleuca) and the collared flycatcher (F. albicollis). In May, they set up nest-box traps occupied by dummy male birds. Some of the nest boxes broadcast recordings of flycatcher song, while others remained silent. Normally, male flycatchers arrive at the nest site earlier than females, establish and defend a small territory, and sing frequently from a perch near the nest hole. When the researchers checked their nest boxes, they found that nine of the ten trapped flycatchers were in nest boxes with the 'singing' dummy males, which seems to indicate what amateur ornithologists have thought all along.

New Scientist, No. 1544, 22 January 1987, p. 28.

Tasks 7 and 8

1. Seeing things only in terms of their function. The boxes are seen as containers, not as potential supports.
2. To mount three candles vertically on a soft wooden screen using any object on the table.
3. For one group the candles, matches and tacks were presented in their boxes. For the other, these boxes were presented alongside their contents, but not as containers.
4. 41% of the first group solved the problem. 86% of the second group solved the problem.
5. Functional fixity can hinder problem solving by preventing us thinking of uses for objects other than their normal function.
6. The extra objects distracted the subjects.

The only information which cannot be derived directly from these samples is the result for the second group, but this can be inferred.

FUNCTIONAL FIXITY: A BARRIER TO CREATIVE PROBLEM SOLVING

The German psychologist Karl Duncker first proposed the concept of functional fixity about 1930, and he illustrated it with a few simple experiments. Because these experiments were done with so few

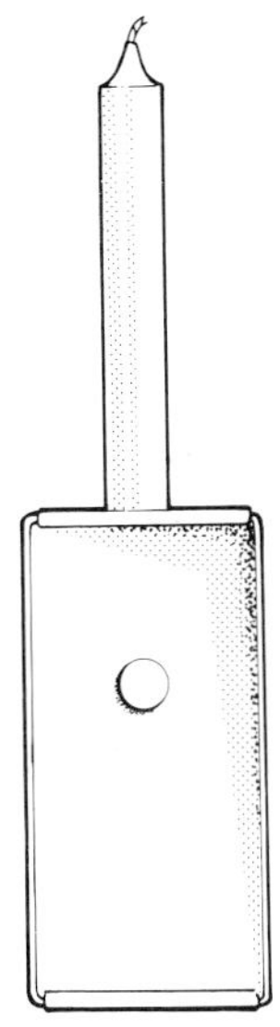

Figure C

subjects, several American psychologists repeated them, and they obtained results similar to Duncker's. R. E. Adamson at Stanford University did one such experiment.

The task: Mount three candles vertically on a soft wooden screen, using any object on the table. Among the objects are three cardboard boxes and a number of matches and thumbtacks. *The solution:* Mount one candle on each box by melting wax on the box and sticking the candle to it; then tack the boxes to the screen (see Figure C).

For one group (twenty-nine college students), the candles, matches, and tacks were placed *in* the three boxes before they were presented to the subjects (Figure A). *The boxes were thus seen functioning as containers;* whereas in the solution of the problem the boxes would have to be seen as supports or shelves. For the second group (twenty-eight subjects), the boxes were empty and placed among the other objects (Figure B). There the boxes were not seen functioning as containers. Twenty minutes were allowed for the solution.

Of the first group, only twelve of the subjects (or 41 percent) were able to solve the problem: apparently the remaining subjects in this group could not perceive the boxes with the meaning of platform or shelf. Of the second group, twenty-four (or 86 percent) were able to solve the problem.

These results give striking evidence that functional fixity may be an important barrier in creative problem solving. Note also the mental dazzle operating here, as a result of the useless, hence distracting, extra objects.

R. E. ADAMSON. Functional fixedness as related to problem-solving, *Journal of Experimental Psychology*, 1952, 44, 288–291.

Task 9

1. they do not require expensive interviewers.
2. questionnaires are cheap.
3. they may not be reliable.
4. many people do not return them.

Task 10

1. a
2. b
3. a
4. a

Task 11

For example
In contrast
For instance
However
Furthermore
In other words

Task 12

drawbacks – noun – *disadvantages, limitations*
spontaneous – adjective – *unplanned, immediate, without thinking*
ambiguity – noun – *when the meaning of words is unclear because they can be understood in different ways*
independent – adjective – *free-standing, without connection with other answers*

Task 13

1. flexible – *adaptable* – 'can be altered'
2. candid – *frank* – 'since . . . not have to commit themselves'
3. insincere – *not genuine* – 'distinguish between a genuine . . .'
4. anticipate – *predict* – 'look ahead'
5. restricting – *limiting* – 'problem . . . full notes . . . solved . . . marks or numbers'
6. inkling – *hint* – 'tone . . . way . . . appearance, dress and accent' (all very indirect)
7. anonymous – *without identification* – 'but not if identification is required'
8. misheard – *misunderstood* – 'fill in their own . . . and so cannot be . . .'

Task 16

Rapid revolution is the answer

CYCLISTS who want both speed and endurance should pedal faster, according to Anthony Sargeant, of the Academic Medical Centre in Amsterdam. He has found that the optimum pedalling rate is about 100 rpm. Muscle physiologists previously thought that the optimum rate was much lower at about 60 rpm. Sargeant studied the performance of a group of men on exercise bicycles which only allowed them to pedal at a fixed rate He found that cyclists get maximum power output, for short periods, at about 115 revolutions per minute.

Cyclists can pedal longer if they are not using their maximum available force in each pedal stroke. They can use half the force in each stroke if they pedal twice as fast. But cyclists cannot get as much power behind each push if the pedals are moving very fast. This limits the optimum rate to below 115 rpm. Sargeant found that cyclists pedalling at 40 rpm use 70 per cent of their total available power and those pedalling at 99 rpm only use 46 per cent and so have greater endurance. □

New Scientist, No. 1618, 23 June 1988, p. 44.

Small and mighty fibres

THE STRUCTURE of muscle in migratory birds is related to the distance they migrate. According to Björn Lundgren, of Uppsala University in Sweden, and Karl-Heinz Kiessling of the Swedish University of Agricultural Sciences, those species that travel long distances have fibres that are much smaller than those that do not migrate.

Muscle fibres are surrounded by tiny blood vessels. The smaller the fibre, the shorter the distance that oxygen and nutrients have to travel to reach it becomes. So it is easier for the muscle with small fibres to endure prolonged work as oxygen is more readily available. Changes in the size of fibres and in the blood supply may be an adaptation to the demands of migration (*Journal of Comparative Physiology*, vol 158, p 165).

The researchers looked at the types of fibres, and at the supply of blood to these fibres, in 15 species, either during migration or during the breeding season. Some of these birds, such as the sand martin, migrate over long distances; others migrate over short distances.

All of the species had muscle fibres that were capable of endurance; but two species—robins and blackbirds—also had some fibres that specialised in generating rapid force without oxygen.

It is surprising, the researchers say, that a bird like a robin should have these fast fibres, because even much larger birds can manage to take off without them. □

New Scientist, No. 1633, 8 October 1988, p. 28.

Healthy advice for economy class high-flyers

IF YOU want to avoid dropping dead on a long aeroplane flight, stay off alcohol, forget cigarettes and take a wander up and down the aisle from time to time. That's the advice of John Cruikshank, a cardiovascular consultant to ICI Pharmaceuticals in Cheshire.

By following the same advice, you can steer clear of puffy legs and ankles, say Cruikshank and colleagues in *The Lancet*

(27 August, p 497). All three authors have personal experience of discomfort brought on by the cramped conditions typical of economy class travel aboard aeroplanes.

Cruikshank fell foul of aircraft travel during a series of lengthy trips to the Far East. He ended up in hospital with pneumonia.

The problem is, he explains, that in such cramped conditions, the circulation becomes so sluggish that blood cells aggregate into clots which cause swollen calves and ankles.

The swelling explains, he says, why people sometimes find it difficult to put shoes back on after long flights.

Worse still, fragments of the clots can break off and migrate to blood vessels around the heart and lungs. Here, they could potentially kill.

The authors point out that "over a three-year period at Heathrow Airport, 18 per cent of the 61 sudden deaths in long-distance passengers were due to pulmonary embolus (a clot in the lung)".

Cruikshank and colleagues recommend that airlines warn passengers to exercise on long flights and to avoid alcohol. Exercise will prevent clots from forming. Abstinence prevents dehydration, another contributory factor.

As an aside, the authors point out that short people are especially at risk. This, says Cruikshank, is because they are more likely to rest their calves on the seats during the journey. So too are people who have a history of problems with veins, or with previous trauma or heart failure. □

New Scientist, No. 1629, 8 September 1988, p. 38.

The origin of arthritis

RHEUMATOID arthritis may have originated in the New World long before it first appeared in Europe and other parts of the Old World.

Bruce Rothschild of the Arthritis Center of Northeastern Ohio, and Kenneth Turner and Michael DeLuca of the University of Alabama have found evidence of rheumatoid arthritis in the skeletons of six prehistoric native Americans who lived during the so-called Late Archaic cultural period, 3000 to 5000 years ago (*Science*, vol 241, p 1498).

The researchers speculate that the disease crossed the Atlantic some time after the first European contact with the New World in 1492. They say that the disease could have spread with people, tobacco, deer, rodents or dogs, all of which were associated with early transatlantic trade.

Rothschild and his colleagues base their claim on the discovery of areas of diseased bone tissue in two male and four female adult skeletons from Late Archaic sites along the Tennessee River in northwestern Alabama. The types of lesions, their

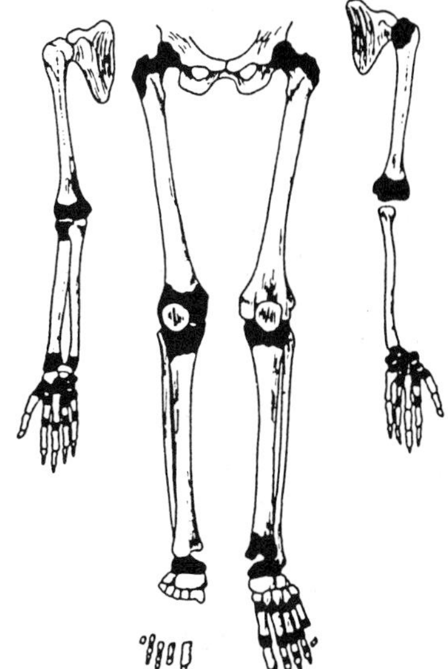

Fossil evidence suggests that arthritis is an old problem

distribution at the joints and their radiological appearance are strikingly similar to the conditions seen in patients with rheumatoid arthritis today. □

New Scientist, No. 1634, 15 October 1988, p. 33.

Unit 4 The developing world

Task 3

a) Natural resources *or* Health, food and nutrition
b) Trade *or* Economic development
c) Health, food and nutrition *or* Demography, population and migration
d) Trade
e) Trade
f) Education and training *or* Women and minorities

Task 4

The main points are all signposted:

- '*One of the most important* problems facing developing countries today is the rapid increase in population.' (lines 1–2)
- '*The main point to be made here* is that more and more people are concentrated in those countries which are least able to provide a living for them.' (lines 5–7)
- '*What is responsible for this population rise is not . . . but* a sharp decline in the death rate in developing countries.' (lines 8–9)

– '*The main reason* for the reduction in the death rate in the developing world has been improved public health measures.' (lines 16–17)
– '*In other words*, the death rate can be cut without anything else changing.' (lines 24–5)

Task 5

Only *For example* (line 6) marks an unimportant point. All the other signposts indicate important points, although of the three reasons given, the third is clearly marked as the most important (line 10).

Task 8

Text 1
First category: *Long-term causes of household income loss or income instability which increase vulnerability of poor people*
Causes:
1. *environmental degradation*
2. *social changes*

Example of social changes: *breakdown of traditional social obligations to the poor*

Text 2
Secondary category: *Precipitating factors setting off the secondary events which worsen the situation*
Types of precipitating factors:
1. *those which reduce the food supply*
2. *those which it is feared will do so*
3. *those which reduce the purchasing power of the poor*

Example of secondary events: *spiralling food prices*

Text 3
Third category: *Relief failure, i.e. governmental famine-prevention administration which is inadequate, incompetent or unable to operate*
Example of relief failure: *Sudan and Ethiopia (delays in relief)*
Example of relief success: *Bangladesh in the early 1980s*

Task 9

1. the transfer of medical technology
2. bad manpower planning
3. large-scale capital-intensive projects
4. spraying against malaria
5. social change
6. rapid inflation
7. parts of Africa
8. remove the underlying causes of famine

Task 10

1. inflation
2. injustice of man or the injustice of nature
3. water shortage
4. the pressure of population
5. drought, floods, war and epidemics
6. rising food prices
7. administrative incompetence
8. the pressure of a rapidly rising population
9. capital-intensive projects
10. poverty

Task 11

cause + START	*cause* + MORE
create	increase
set off	raise
dislodge	double

cause + LESS	*cause* + HARM
reduce	aggravate
halve	worsen
restrict	impair
cut	
lower	

Task 12

1. a
2. c
3. b
4. a
5. b

Unit 5 The natural world

Task 2

Even the best protected habitats are vulnerable.
Many animals need a wide territory. If this is reduced, in the long term, inbreeding will cause extinction.
For larger animals, captive breeding is essential.

Task 4

The amount provided by the reader will depend on his or her knowledge of the world.

2. Because in the Sahel there is poverty, hunger and/or civil war.
3. Because of inbreeding. The genetic pool will not be large enough to ensure a vigorous population.
4. Breeding in zoos.
5. Because they require a very large habitat. Hence their habitat is most at risk. Large animals are also more vulnerable to hunting.

Tasks 5 and 6

1. equals, is equal to, is
2. is more than, greater than
3. is less than
4. very, greatly
5. leads to, causes, results in, is the cause of
6. is caused by, results from, is the effect of
7. possibly
8. unlikely
9. regarding, with reference to
10. etcetera, and so on, and other things
11. that is to say, they are, namely
12. compare
13. work cited, book previously mentioned
14. note well
15. circa, about
16. Food and Agricultural Organisation
17. government – first syllable, last letter
18. hypothetical – important syllables
19. probably – first syllable only
20. important – first syllable only
21. limited – key consonants
22. standard – key consonants
23. very – first letter
24. discussion – *ion* ending becomes *n*

Task 8

Text 1 – Leigh
Objectives:
1. *Learn full effects exploitatn*
2. *Demonstrate benefits from unexploited state and maximise benefits*

Criteria for selecting the reserve: *Representative of wide area biologically & levels of exploitatn*
Rules: *No fishing, no removal of animals, no disturbance*
Achievements: *Increase in visitors, active research site*
Disadvantages: *Specific reasons for ban could not be given*

Text 2 – Poor Knights
Objectives: *Establish working reserve without antagonising existing users*
Criteria for selecting the reserve: *Scenically & biologically special, remote from human activity*
Rules: *Eliminate activities known to cause damage; protect all other interests*
Achievements: *Successful as holding action*
Disadvantages: *No clear principle for public support; complex rules; difficult to change them; people with rights of access become defensive*

Task 11

	Paragraph(s)
Introduction	Para. A
The laboratory	Para. B Para. C Para. F Para. G
The forest	Para. D Para. E
The political arena	Para. H Para. I

Task 12

Here are some sample answers:

The laboratory:
Microbiologists / identify all strains . . . / develop a vaccine / effective treatment / drug / trospectomycin / bacteria
Biologists / investigating the . . . highly specialised digestive system / could lead to improved diets / dietary supplements / Experts at the University . . . and the . . . Zoo . . . have created a 'koala biscuit'

The forest:
Ecologists / field data / wild koalas / forests / sparsely wooded areas / 'quality' habitat / eucalyptus

The political arena:
Wildlife officers / city planners / force people to / bylaws / conservationists / city, state and federal governments / protect

Task 13

a) all chlamydia strains
b) vaccine
c) treatment
d) overpop. to underpop. areas
e) sustain koala pop.
f) koala's highly spec. digest. system for better understanding of nutritional requirements
g) dietary supplements
h) safeguard koala colonies on their land
i) 'build' koalas into rapidly expandg communities
j) dog and human activities in koala country
k) protect koala habitat

Task 14

The developing world c, f, i, k, o
The natural world b, e, g, l, n, i (possible)
The spirit of enquiry a, d, h, j, m

Task 16

a) essential
b) inbreeding, infertile/poor stock
c) not sufficient
d) poverty, political instability
e) sustain sufficient number of animals
f) desirable
g) essential

Task 17

Title = Is breeding which involves the computerisation of animal data and inter-zoo cooperation on a large scale (to guarantee the best possible genetic combinations) the most successful way to handle the problem of wildlife conservation?

We can infer that the author hopes for success for this programme from these lines:
'*Breeding in zoos has become an* essential *part of conservation but* unless *such breeding is carried out on a large scale* . . . it would be bound to fail.' (lines 5–9)
'*It is clear that even if the best efforts are made to save what is left of the wilderness*, many animals . . . *will* still be doomed.' (lines 35–38)
'*For many creatures captive breeding might be desirable. For many of the bigger ones in particular,* it is now essential.' (lines 38–40)

Unit 6 The physical world

Task 1

The diagram shows a survival still suitable for use in deserts and semi-deserts. A shallow pit is dug and lined with any plant materials available. A small container is placed in the pit to collect any moisture. Plastic sheet is stretched over the pit and held in place by stones round the edge of the pit. A single stone is placed in the centre of the sheet, above the container, to act as a weight. Water evaporates from the plant material and condenses on the sheet. Because of the weight, it runs down the sheet and collects in the container.

Task 2

a) table
b) graph
c) flowchart
d) schematic diagram
e) piechart
f) horizontal bar chart
g) vertical bar chart

Note that a bar chart and histogram (example on page 70) are similar in that information is shown in blocks, but differ in that the blocks are self-contained pieces of information in bar charts, but in histograms the data is continuous.

Task 3 (Examples)

a) *Specific:* 4006 ha of broad-leaved forest in the tropical Americas were destroyed each year between 1981 and 1985.
Main: The rate of destruction of tropical forests is increasing.
b) *Specific:* None (no quantities are given).
Main: As the land becomes desert, yield falls.
c) *Specific:* The first stage in the planning process is to identify the problems.
Main: The planning process has eight stages. The initial and final stages are influenced by the values and perceptions of the planner.
d) *Specific:* The lithosphere is about 60 km in depth.
Main: The physical world consists of the lithosphere, the hydrosphere, the biosphere and the atmosphere.
e) *Specific:* 25.1% of the world's population in 2100 will be East Asian.

Main: The most important changes in the composition of the world's population in 2100 will be the increase in the South Asian proportion and the reduction in the North American, USSR and European proportion.

f) *Specific:* 50% of US consumption of lead in 1970 was recycled.
Main: With the exception of lead and antimony, between 10 and 25% of the major metals used in the USA in 1979 were recycled.

g) *Specific:* 66% of the population of rural Asia are not served with water.
Main: The urban population of the developing world are much better served with water than the rural population.

Task 4

1. igneous intrusion, volcanic plug
2. eroded by ice
3. streamlined by the ice flow
4. softer sandstone protected by the crag and boulder clay deposited by the ice

Task 5

1. transpiration is from plants, evaporation is from soil and water
2. water which is not absorbed but runs off the land to the sea in the form of rivers
3. by infiltration
4. evaporation
5. water from volcanic steam
6. the level below which the ground is saturated

Task 6

Cheapest method of evaporation

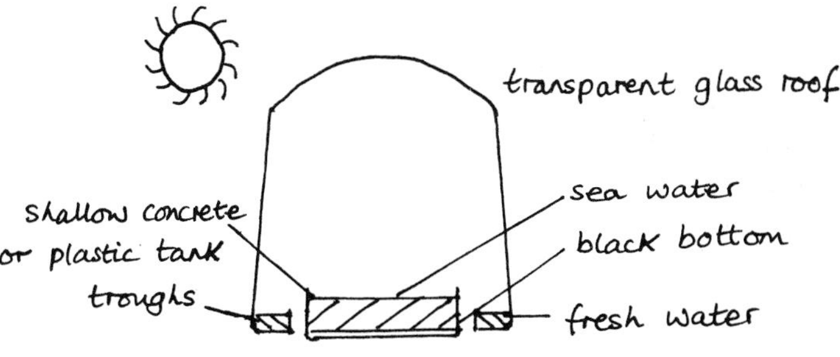

'Arizona method'

1
Sea water pumped to installation

2
warmed by sun or 'waste heat' from diesel generator

3
fresh water evaporates

4
condenses because cooled by cold sea water

5
irrigates plants in closed plastic greenhouses (inflated bags)

6
transpired water trapped and recycled

Task 7

Check these approximate meanings with dictionary definitions.

1. *brasses:* musical instruments played by blowing air in the mouthpiece and vibrating the lips; they have long hollow bodies
2. *eddy:* a movement of air
3. *cavities:* hollow places like the mouth and nose

Task 8

violin, strings, bridge, f-holes, front (top) plate, back plate, body resonances, string frequencies, distorted

Task 9

1. If they could be transported to the area.
2. Providing they had an atmosphere and climate similar to our own.
3. If deserts could be cultivated, more food could be produced.
4. Providing the resources existed for their construction.
5. If we could be persuaded to recycle such a high percentage of glass.

Task 10

Liquid fresh water supply	*Volume (km³)*	*% of world total*
N. American large lakes	32,000	25
African large lakes	36,000	30
Lake Baikal	22,000	18
Large lakes in other continents	3,000	2
Rivers and lesser lakes	32,000	25
TOTAL	125,000	

Note: The volume of rivers and lesser lakes is by inference.
Main idea: 75% of the world's liquid fresh water supply is in large lakes.

Unit 7 Into the future

Task 5

Similarities: In both surveys approximately 44% feel that the benefits of science outweigh the negative aspects.
Differences: The phrasing of the questions; the presentation of the results – the scales used.

Task 8

C, B, D, A

Para. A starts with '*But . . .*' and Para. B starts '*Such a present . . .*' Both clearly refer to earlier text, hence neither paragraph can begin the text.

Para. C refers to '*a present*' which suggests that Para. C precedes B. In Para. A, '*this information*' indicates that A follows D where the '*information*' is described.

At first glance either Para. C or D could begin the text but in Para. D the words '*the project aims to produce just such a generalised genome*' make it clear that Para. D follows B where the '*generalised genome*' is first mentioned.

Task 9

Introduction:
Definition of genome: *personal record of DNA that moulds physical/mental characteristics*
'generalised genome': *cf. generalised skeleton, needed by medical science*

Description of 'Human genome project':
Cost: *£2 billion*
Timescale: *15 years +*
Aims: *establish generalised genome*
Applications by:
a) geneticists: *establish differences between indiv. and norm*
b) biochemists: *plan bioengineered organisms to produce useful human proteins & hormones*
c) doctors and researchers: *discover, diagnose, treat genetic diseases*

Problem:
Quantity of information: *volume of data will make it difficult to process*

Task 10

C, B, A

In Para. A, references to '*tentative suggestion*' and '*it*' make it unlikely that this is the first paragraph.

Para. C ends with a discussion of cost, while Para. B begins with reference to cost. This topic link helps indicate that C precedes B.

Task 11

Aims: *map & sequence human genome*
Definition: *the DNA in all 24 chromosomes*
Timescale: *15 years*
Cost: *$3 billion*
cf. Physical science projects: *e.g. $30 billion for space station*
Biologists' attitudes to program: *exhilaration vs fear for small science biology*
Reasons for adoption of program: *technically just feasible, US legislators keen to boost US competitiveness in biotechnology*

There is little difference in factual information, but there is a slight difference in emphasis. Text 1 gives more detail on the kind and quantity of information the project will yield, the applications and the problem of so much information. Text 2 gives more information on comparative costs, the status of the project, the reasons for its adoption and the implications for biology. Reading and comparing both texts should provide a broader understanding of the programme. As the basic facts agree, we can conclude that the texts are probably reliable.

Task 12

1. 2	5. 3
2. 1	6. 4
3. 1	7. 1
4. 6	

Task 13

5, 6, 7, 3, 2, 1, 4

Task 14

Text topic: Britain and the human genome

Introduction: Definition US commitment Expected cost	*Para. 1*
UK contribution: UK funding	*Para. 2/3*
Reasons for UK involvement	*Para. 4*
Strengths of UK approach	*Para. 5*
Recommended strategy	*Para. 6*

Unit 8 The individual and society

Task 1

Facts can be verified by experiment or by reference to other facts. They are true statements supported by evidence. This does not mean that every statement presented as a fact is true. Facts can also change when new evidence becomes available. Opinions are personal beliefs. They are subjective.

This task is to promote discussion. There is room for disagreement in this division.
Facts: 1, 8, 9
Opinions: 2, 3, 4, 5, 6, 7, 10

Task 5

Text 1

1. Most learning NOT because teaching.
2. ALTHO' Teaching may help in s. conditions.
3. BUT Most knowledge out/s school.
4. & In/s school only insofar as confined there.
5. Most learning casual (not intentional).
6. e.g. 1st lang. learnt casually.
7. Even most intentional learning NOT because teaching.
8. e.g. If 2nd lang. learnt well, learnt because odd circumstances like travel.
9. ALSO Fluent reading because out/s school activities.
10. Good readers merely believe learned at school.

LIVERPOOL
JOHN MOORES UNIVERSITY
AVRIL ROBARTS LRC
TEL. 0151 231 4022

11. BUT When challenged, discard this illusion.

Almost all points are assertions.

Text 2

1. Equal obligatory schooling is economically unfeasible.
2. ∵ In Latin America 350/1,500 × more public money spent on graduate student than median citizen.
3. & In US discrimination worse.
4. ∵ Richest educate children privately.
5. & Richest obtain 10 × more per capita public money than poorest.
6. ∵ Rich children longer at school.
7. & University year more expensive than school year.
8. & Most private universities depend on tax-derived finances.

Task 7

Conclusion to Texts 1 and 2 on marriage:
If there are winners and losers in marriage, it is hard to avoid the conclusion that men are more often the winners and women the losers.

Task 8

1. a
2. a
3. a
4. a
5. b
6. b

Task 9

Maximisers	*Minimisers*
completely (1)	only (4)
in all respects (3)	simply (7)
altogether (6)	at least to some extent (14)
entirely (8)	merely (16)
much (9)	hardly (17)
fully (12)	
quite (15)	

Task 11

Text 1

Opinion	*Divorce due conflict between economic system and family.*
Supporting reasons	*Industry needs cheap female labour.* *Media creates demand for goods.* *Both spouses must work to purchase goods.* *But wife still expected to do housework and raise children.* *And be subservient to husband.* *Even though sharing economic burden.*
Conclusion	*Conflict between spouses results.* *Leads to divorce.*

Text 2

Statement	*Each time divorce laws eased, divorce rate increases.*
Possible explanations and argument against	*Higher divorce rate because more marital instability.* *But how know which came first?* *Permissive laws cause breakdown.* *But would happily married divorce because of new law?*
Explanation of writer	*New laws provide solution to problems of unhappily married.*
Explanation repeated	*Changes in law do not cause breakdowns; provide solutions.*

Unit 9 Work

Tasks 3 and 4

	Text 1	*Text 2*
NATURE OF WORK	*A curse*	*Essential, a social activity*
EFFECT OF WORKING CONDITIONS	*Reduce dislike Improve mechanical efficiency*	*No direct effect on morale but can affect health and comfort*
MOTIVATION FOR WORK	*Money and fear of unemployment*	*Money unimportant Fear of unemployment because it cuts man off from society*

Task 7

Text 1
If working time falls, then *people will work less*. The result will be *more employment*. Working time will fall because of *the shorter working week*, longer holidays, earlier retirement, more sabbaticals and *job-sharing*. This means a mix of part-time paid and part-time unpaid work will become more common but *it will not restore full employment*. The first reason is that the reduction of working time cannot take place on a scale and at a pace sufficient to *create work for all who want it*. The second reason is that if *it could be done on such a scale and at such a pace*, it would create a situation where full employment would no longer be the main form of work.

Task 8

1. IF working time falls THEN *people will work less*
2. THEREFORE *there will be more employment*
3. Working time will fall
   BECAUSE OF *the shorter working week*
4. longer holidays
5. *earlier retirement*
6. more sabbaticals
7. AND *job-sharing*
8. THEREFORE *a mix of part-time paid and unpaid work will become more common*
9. BUT *it will not restore full employment*
10. BECAUSE the scale and pace are insufficient
11. and BECAUSE IF *it could be done on such a scale and at such a pace* THEN full employment would no longer be the only form of work

Task 10

Text 2
It may seem that if working hours are cut by 10 to 20%, then *mass unemployment will fall*. But labour will not accept wage cuts on such a scale. If wage cuts are imposed, *there will be serious social upheaval*. If hours are cut but wages maintained, Britain will be unable to compete in world markets because her goods will be so expensive. Even if Britain's goods could be sold, unemployment would not fall because of *its geographical distribution* and the mismatch between the skills the unemployed can offer and the skills required for modern employment.

Shortening working hours has value because *we still get psychological benefits* from employment even when we work less. Cutting hours will improve the quality of working life for the employed but *it is a slow way to reduce unemployment*.

Task 11

1. IF working hours are cut THEN *mass unemployment will fall*
2. BUT labour will not accept wage cuts on such a scale
3. IF *wage cuts are imposed* THEN there will be serious social upheaval
4. IF *hours are cut but wages maintained* THEN Britain will be unable to compete in world markets
5. BECAUSE her goods will be so expensive
6. IF Britain's goods could be sold THEN *unemployment would not fall*
7. BECAUSE OF its geographical distribution

8. AND *the mismatch between skills offered and required*
9. *Shortening working hours has value* BECAUSE we get the psychological benefits of work even when we work less
10. THEREFORE cutting working hours will improve the quality of life for the employed
11. BUT *it is a slow way to reduce unemployment*

Task 14

Each argument contains a flaw.

Text 1
The argument appears to be well-constructed but would you accept that women strike more than men because they are more emotional? The statement on which the argument is based is false.

Text 2
B happens after A. Therefore A causes B. Because two actions happen in sequence does not mean that the first causes the second. After you take medicine, you may recover from an illness but was it the medicine which made you better or would you have recovered in any case?

Text 3
A is true in one situation. Therefore A is true in all situations. Such arguments are often used to justify importing foreign solutions to solve local problems.

Text 4
A is like B in some ways. Therefore A is like B in all ways. This argument is often used to make false parallels with situations which are similar in some aspects but very different in others.

Text 5
A is true because an authority says so. Appeals to philosophical, religious and political 'truths' are often used to justify unacceptable conclusions.

Text 6
A is true once. Therefore A is always true. No scientist would accept a conclusion based on only one observation. In this argument there is simply not enough evidence to support such a major claim.

Text 7
This is a circular argument. Saying the same thing twice does not make it true. The writer does not present an argument. The opening statement is merely repeated in different words.

Task 15

1. emphasis
2. distancing
3. emphasis
4. emphasis
5. emphasis
6. distancing

Task 17

1. and 2. The question mark in the title indicates the writer's doubts about this goal.
4. Unemployed people would feel resentful because they would feel their lives had no value. This is because most people have no tradition of leisure, but on the contrary feel the need to work and be useful.
5. The employed would be resentful because they would feel they had to support the idle.
7. A secure minimum wage for the unemployed.
8. A society in which citizens could choose their own mix of paid and unpaid work.
9. '*did come*' instead of 'came' emphasises the writer's belief that it will not happen.
   '*one thing is sure*' emphasises his next point.
   '*in fact*' gives further emphasis.
   '*in other words*' restates his point, giving further emphasis and clarity.
   '*at least to some extent*' hedges his conclusion.

Unit 10 Using reference sources (1)

Task 1 (Examples)

1. an encyclopaedia
2. an atlas, a gazeteer
3. any source of up-to-date statistics, e.g. *The Statesman's Year Book*
4. a specialist encyclopaedia in either psychology or language
5. a specialist bibliography
6. as 3

7. a dictionary of biography, an encyclopaedia
8. a dictionary
9. a specialist dictionary of computing or technology

Task 2

1. definitions of technical terms
2. very wide coverage of all aspects of knowledge
3. up-to-date definitions, examples of use, grammatical information, pronunciation, illustrations
4. up-to-date information on all the countries of the world, their political systems, trade, population, etc.
5. a bibliography of writing on women
6. a wide-ranging reference on all aspects of language
7. up-to-date statistics on trade, education, health and many other aspects of all UN member states
8. wide coverage of all aspects of knowledge, not so comprehensive as *Britannica*, with a US slant
9. help on locating places and natural features throughout the world
10. information on the lives of famous people of all ages and times, especially Americans

Task 3

1. 2, 8	6. 4
2. 9	7. 2, 8
3. 4, 7	8. 3
4. 6	9. 1
5. 5	10. 1, 7

Task 4

1. 1860s
2. American Seventhday Adventists
3. flaked, puffed, shredded, granular
4. the final stage
5. advertising – diversification and promotion
6. *not stated*
7. children

Task 5

1. Which science used radiocarbon dating?
2. Where can we find further information about radiocarbon dating?
3. When does an organism cease to absorb carbon dioxide?
4. What does B.P. mean in the context of radiocarbon dating?
5. What is the 'preferred half-life' for carbon fourteen?
6. Why is there a lack of correlation between tree-ring dating and radiocarbon dating?

Answers

1. archaeology
2. T. Watkins, *Radiocarbon: Calibration and Prehistory*, Edinburgh, 1975
3. on death
4. before present
5. 5,730 years
6. the production of carbon fourteen has not been constant throughout time

Task 6

1. China, India, Indonesia
2. North Korea
3. Bangladesh, Burma, Japan, Nepal
4. There has been no significant change in rice production between 1985 and 1988.
5. Area of land under rice cultivation was reduced.
6. The production figures are unofficial.
7. In the period 1979 to 1988 the area under cultivation did not change, while production increased by around 20%.

Task 8

Klein and Richards focus on reading. Barrass, Palmer, and Open University will contain general study skills advice which should include reading.

Task 10

1. e	4. a	7. g
2. b	5. f	
3. d	6. c	

Task 11

1. Brittain, possibly Byrne, Oates & Williamson
2. Signs
3. Blackstone, Deem, possibly Sharpe
4. Shaw
5. Graham, Roby

Task 12

1. C659
2. C661
3. C656, 664, 665
4. C666
5. C668
6. C666, 667
7. C657
8. C662

Task 14

Americana only: schools attended, vagabond after war, stage debut
Britannica only: cause of stiff upper lip, early screen career, characters played in films
They disagree on his date of birth (Americana gives Jan. 23, 1899, Britannica Dec. 25, 1899), on the date of *The Maltese Falcon* (Americana gives 1942, Britannica 1941), and on the date of *To Have and Have Not* (Americana gives 1945, Britannica 1944).

Task 15

Humphrey Bogart

Dates, birthplace: *23/1/1899* or *25/12/1899 (New York) – 14/1/1957*

Early life: *school in New York and Andover, US Navy in World War 1, vagabond after war*

Early acting career: *juvenile roles in comedies, breakthrough in gangster role in 1935*

Significant films:
High Sierra, 1941
Casablanca, 1942
The African Queen, 1951, etc.

Type of character played: *'tough guy'*

Task 17

Text 1

1. How FLL happens according to behaviourists: *'In this view, FLL is seen . . .'* (line 3)
2. Influence of L1: *'Properties of the L1 are thought to exercise an influence . . .'* (line 7)
3. Aim of behaviourist teaching: *'The main aim of behaviourist teaching . . .'* (line 25)
4. Problems with the behaviourist view: *'There are several problems . . .'* (line 29)
5. Two problems with imitation: *'Imitation alone . . .'* (line 30)
   'Nor does imitation . . .' (line 35)
6. Evidence from research: *'In a frequently-cited early study . . .'* (line 40)
7. Conclusion: *'The systematic comparison of . . .'* (line 54)

Text 2

1. The cognitive view: *'In this view, . . .'* (line 3)
2. Definition of interlanguage: *'At each stage, . . .'* (line 10)
3. Role of error analysis: *'Error analysis plays a central role . . .'* (line 14)
4. Importance of errors: *'The errors provide positive evidence . . .'* (line 18)
5. Complexity of error analysis: *'However, the analysis of errors turns out to be a highly complex matter . . .'* (line 31)
6. Limitations of error analysis: *'However, as with contrastive analysis, the approach cannot . . .'* (line 67)
7. Scope of new explanatory models: *'To understand the way languages . . .'* (line 75)

Theories of Language Acquisition

Theory – Behaviourist

When influential: *1950s, 1960s*

Learning takes place through:
1. *Imitation*
2. *Reinforcement*

L1 influences L2 learning by positive transfer (similarities) and negative transfer (differences)

Errors: *Caused by L1 interference*

Teaching aim: *Form new correct habits through intensive practice, eliminate interference errors*

Problems:
1. *Imitation cannot provide for creativity in language*
2. *Imitation does not explain how learners behave*
3. *Contrastive analysis cannot predict or explain more than a small part of errors and difficulties*

Theory – Cognitive

When influential: *1970s on*

Learning takes place through:

1. *Forming hypotheses about the structure of L2*
2. *Constructing and trying out rules*
3. *A series of transitional stages when learner's language = interlanguage (neither L1 nor L2)*

Errors: *Evidence of learning taking place*

Problems:

1. *Errors are also due to L1, teaching, materials, need to communicate with limited resources*
2. *Not all errors are equally systematic and disruptive, e.g. vocabulary errors are less predictable, yet more disruptive*
3. *Learner's intentions are often unknown therefore difficult to identify nature of the error*

Unit 11 Using reference sources (2)

Task 2

7

Task 4

1. Proper names of people, countries and concepts which are used to classify information.
2. References that direct the user from terms not used to those under which entries can be found.
3. References that guide the user to other connected terms that might be useful.
4. References which direct the user to a range of other possible headings or subheadings. They also remind the user that information can be found under similar headings, for example 'Law' and 'Legal'.

Task 5

1. *Folklore*
2. Fairies and the folklore of disability; Changelings, hybrids and the solitary fairy
3. Susan Eberly
4. Relationship between changeling lore and children born with congenital disorders
5. Vol. 99
6. Changelings

Task 6

Languages: Study and Teaching: Great Britain

Task 7

A Life Sciences
B Arts and Humanities
C Social and Behavioural Sciences

A *Current Contents: Life Sciences*, Vol. 33, No. 24, 11 Dec. 1990.
B *Current Contents: Arts and Humanities*, Vol. 12, No. 26, 17 Dec. 1990.
C *Current Contents: Social and Behavioural Sciences*, Vol. 22, No. 51, 17 Dec. 1990.

Task 8

CC pg 40	J Pg 443
CC pg 40	J Pg 445
CC pg 50	J Pg 574

Task 9

Your institution may prescribe different forms of referencing. This is modern bibliographical format:

Coleman, D.W. (1990) Guest Editorial, *Simulation and Gaming*, Vol. 21, No. 4, p. 443.

Baltra, A. (1990) Language Learning Through Computer Games, *Simulation and Gaming*, Vol. 21, No. 4, p. 445.

Rosenberg, S., Huitema, J.S. and Rayner, K. (1990) Reading, Writing and Language Learning, *American Journal of Psychology*, Vol. 103, No. 4, p. 574.

Task 11

1. Quarterly in March, June, September and December
2. Carfax Publishing Company, Abingdon, Oxfordshire, UK
3. To serve the information needs of those concerned with the sociological study of education:

   a) to provide a means of keeping up-to-date with newly published material
   b) to help with retrospective retrieval
4. About 600 journal articles and books each year
5. New Zealand, England, Hong Kong

Task 12

1. f
2. b
3. d
4. e
5. c
6. a

Task 13

334, 038, 205, 417

Task 14

1. C
2. D
3. B
4. A

Acknowledgements

The authors and publishers are grateful to those listed below for permission to reproduce copyright material.

Macmillan Publishers Ltd for the extract on p. 7 from *An Introduction to Insect Pests and their Control* by Peter D. Stiling; Pergamon Press PLC for the extract on p. 8 from *How to Find Out, Printed and On-Line Sources* by G. Chandler, 5th ed., © 1982 and for the extract on p. 14 from *How to find out about engineering* by S.A.J. Parsons, © 1972; BBC Enterprises Ltd for the extract on p. 10 from *The Ascent of Man* by Jacob Bronowski; Macmillan Education Ltd for the extracts on pp. 14–15 and 19–20 from *Studying for a Degree in the Humanities and Social Sciences* by P. Dunleavy and for the extract on pp. 102–3 from *Introductory Sociology* by T. Bilton et al, 2nd ed.; Macdonald & Co. (Publishers) Ltd for the extract on pp. 17–18 from *Learn How to Study, a guide for students of all ages* by D. Rowntree, 3rd ed.; Copp Clark Pitman Ltd for the extract on p. 21, the Contents page from *General Geography* by J. Wreford Watson, Copyright © 1957, Copp Clark Publishing Company Ltd, reprinted by permission of Copp Clark Pitman Ltd; Pan Books Ltd for the extracts on pp. 22–3 from *How to Study* by H. Maddox; Scottish Academic Press Ltd for the extracts on pp. 24–6 from *Encouraging Effective Learning* by A.N. Main; the Tessa Sayle Agency for the extract on pp. 26–7, © by Christopher Parsons, from *How to Study Effectively* (Arrow Books); Professor K.L. Higbee for the extracts on pp. 27–9 from his book *Your Memory, How It Works and How to Improve It* (Prentice-Hall); New Scientist for the extract on pp. 30 and 148 which first appeared in *New Scientist* magazine London, the weekly review of science and technology; Thomas Nelson & Sons Ltd for the extract on pp. 31–3 from *Biology: A Functional Approach* by M.V.B. Roberts; Elsevier Science Publishers Ltd for the Contents page on pp. 41–2 from International Development Abstracts; New Internationalist Publications for the extracts on pp. 42–4; Routledge for the extracts on pp. 47–8 from *Preventing Famine: Policies and Prospects for Africa* by D. Curtis, M. Hubbard and A. Shepherd; Paul Harrison for the extracts on pp. 52–3 from his book *Inside the Third World*, 2nd ed. (Penguin Books); New Scientist, IPC Magazines Ltd and World Press Network © 1990 for the extracts on pp. 40 and 150–1, 57–61, 63–4, 86–7, 88, 89–90 and 93 from articles which first appeared in *New Scientist* magazine, London; Routledge for the flowchart and schematic diagram on p. 68 and the histogram on p. 70 from *Environment and Development* by P. Bartelmus; Croom Helm for the extracts on pp. 70, 74, 75 and 78 from *The Man-Made Future* by C.H. Waddington; Merrill, an imprint of Macmillan Publishing Company, for the extracts on pp. 69, 70 and 73 from *Environmental Geology* by Edward A. Keller, 3rd ed., © 1988, 1985, 1982, 1979, 1976 by Merrill Publishing Company; Chapman & Hall for the extract on p. 72 from *Geology for Civil Engineers* by A.C. McLean and C.D. Gribble (George Allen and Unwin); Edward Arnold for the extract on p. 74 from *A Geology for Engineers* by F.G.H. Blyth and M.H. de Freitas; Methuen & Co. Ltd for the extract on pp. 82–3 from *Water, Earth and Man* by R.J. Chorley; Macmillan Magazines Ltd for the extract on p. 87 from *Nature* vol. 340, p. 11; Marion Boyars Publishers Ltd and Harper & Row, USA, for the extracts on pp. 94–7 from *Deschooling Society* by Ivan Illich; HMSO for the extract on p. 101 from *Social Trends* 20, 1990; Unwin Hyman of Harper Collins Publishers Ltd for the extract on p. 102 from *Sociology, Themes and Perspectives*, 2nd ed., by M. Haralambos; Penguin Books Ltd for the extracts on pp. 105–6 from *The Social Psychology of Industry* by J.A.C. Brown, reproduced by permission of Penguin Books Ltd; Gower Publishing Company Ltd for the extracts on pp. 107 and 113–4 from *Future Work* by James Robertson; Cambridge University Press for the extracts on pp. 108–9 from *Employment and Unemployment* by M. Jahoda and on pp. 127–30 from *The Cambridge Encyclopedia of Language* by D. Crystal; Encyclopaedia Britannica Inc. for the extracts on pp. 116 and 125 reprinted with permission from the *Encyclopaedia Britannica*, 15th ed., © 1986 by Encyclopaedia Britannica, Inc.; Fontana of Harper Collins Publishers Ltd for the extract on p. 117 from *The Fontana Dictionary of Modern Thought*, A. Bullock, A. Stallybrass and S. Trombley (eds); The Macmillan Press Ltd for the extract on p. 118 from *The Statesman's Year Book 1990/91*, 127th ed.; Tavistock Publications for the extract on pp. 121–2 from *Work on Women* by M. Evans and D. Morgan; the American Library Association for the extract on pp. 123–4, reprinted with permission of the American Library Association, from *Sources of Information in the Social Sciences, A Guide to the Literature* by W.H. Webb and Associates, 3rd ed., pp. 204–6, © ALA 1986; Grolier Inc. for the extract on p. 125 from the Encyclopaedia Americana, 1977 Edition, Copyright © 1977 by Grolier Incorporated, reprinted by permission; Bowker Saur for the extracts on pp. 132–7 from the *British Humanities Index*; the Institute for Scientific Information for the extracts on pp. 137–41, reprinted from *Current Contents* with permission of the Institute for Scientific Information ®, © Copyright 1991; and Carfax Publishing Company for the extracts on pp. 141–5 from *Sociology of Education Abstracts*, Vol. 26, No. 2, Journals Oxford Ltd 1990.

It has not been possible to identify/trace the copyright holders of all the material used and in such cases the publishers would welcome information from copyright owners.

Artwork by Wenham Arts.
Book design by Peter Ducker MSTD.